DECORATIVE STENCILS
FOR YOUR HOME

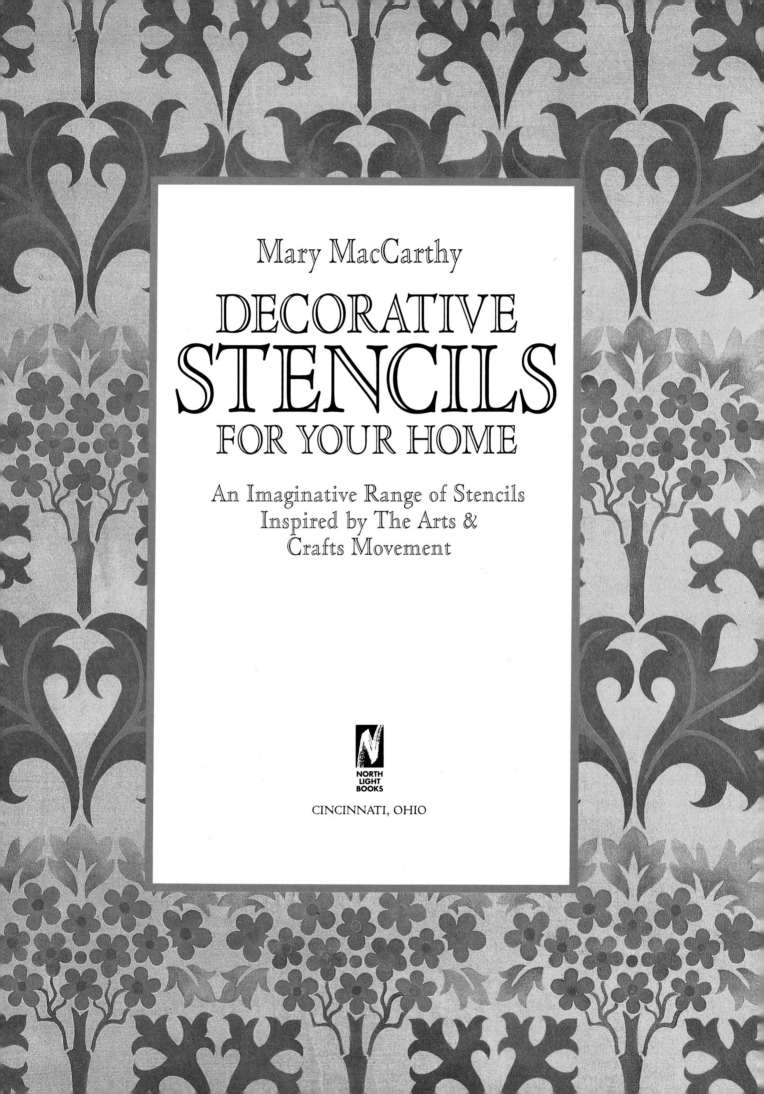

Mary MacCarthy

DECORATIVE STENCILS
FOR YOUR HOME

An Imaginative Range of Stencils
Inspired by The Arts &
Crafts Movement

NORTH
LIGHT
BOOKS

CINCINNATI, OHIO

First published in Great Britain in 1996 by
COLLINS & BROWN LIMITED

First published in North America
in 1996 by North Light Books,
an imprint of F&W Publications, Inc.
1507 Dana Avenue,
Cincinnati, OH 45207
1-800/289-0963

1 3 5 7 9 8 6 4 2

Library of Congress Cataloging-in-Publication Data:
A catalog record for this book
is available.

Conceived, edited and designed by Collins & Brown Limited

EDITORIAL DIRECTOR: *Sarah Hoggett*
ART DIRECTOR: *Roger Bristow*
PROJECT EDITOR: *Alison Wormleighton*
DESIGNER: *Carol McCleeve*
PHOTOGRAPHER: *Lucinda Symons*
STYLIST: *Lucy Elworthy*
ILLUSTRATOR: *Coral Mula*

Reproduction by Master Image, Singapore
Printed and bound in Italy by New Interlitho SpA

CONTENTS

INTRODUCTION

As a child, I would curl up in a large, high-backed armchair with my book and keep very quiet. No one would know I was there. The chair seemed protective, almost magical. Its woven wool cloth depicting large birds surrounded by intertwining leaves and flowers (entitled *The Bird*, as I later learned) was designed by William Morris. Another armchair was covered in a faded red cotton printed with rabbits and thrushes hiding among leaves; this was Morris's *Brother Rabbit* design (shown here). There were also a couple of books which had wonderful decorations and illustrations, like old English fairy tales, that used to fascinate me. I spent hours copying the illustrations of Morris's colleague Walter Crane, my imagination fired by the pictures of knights on horseback and dark-eyed damsels. All of these objects were later to have a major influence on the development of my own work.

In the 1960s I made my first visits to the William Morris Room at the Victoria & Albert Museum in London and began to be aware of Morris's enormous influence on the world of design. It fascinated me that one man could be so creative in so many ways – designing equally well for fabric, paper and glass. Later, as a textile student at Camberwell School of Art & Design, I learned of Morris's poetry, his love of antiquity and his passionate socialism. The realization that creativity could cross so many boundaries was truly inspiring.

The Arts and Crafts movement

Gradually I discovered some of the other members of the Arts and Crafts movement: not only Walter Crane but also William de Morgan, William Burges and Charles Voysey. William Morris was the guiding light of the movement, which took its name from the Arts and Crafts Exhibition Society, with which he was closely involved towards the end of his life. The Society's first exhibition was in 1888, but the real beginning of the movement was around a quarter of a century earlier, when Morris and some friends set up their own firm. Morris was twenty-seven when he founded the firm of Morris, Marshall, Faulkner & Co with the architect Philip Webb, the designer Ford Madox Brown, the painter Edward Burne-Jones and several others. In 1875 the company was reorganized as Morris & Co – although Morris and his friends continued to refer to it simply as the Firm. It continued trading until 1940, forty-four years after Morris's death.

ABOVE

Morris's Brother Rabbit *fabric is one of my earliest childhood memories – it covered one of the armchairs at our house. I have used the rabbit for the garden bench project (shown opposite).*

The Firm took commissions for furniture, stained glass, hand-painted tiles and murals as well as the decoration of interiors. By the late 1860s it was producing printed fabrics and by the early 1870s woven fabrics. Later, carpets, embroidery kits and tapestries were added to the range. (Wallpapers, which were very complex to print, were designed by the Firm and printed elsewhere.)

What all the Arts and Crafts designers had in common was an abhorrence of the meaningless ornament of the Victorians. They believed that materials and function should determine the design of everything. They also hated the shoddy machine-made goods so prevalent then. To them, the Middle Ages, with its craft guilds and lack of machines, represented the golden age of craftsmanship. They advocated a return to the simplicity and decorative honesty of that time. By making hand crafting the means of production, they felt they would be able to bring art to the masses. There would once more be a natural unity between form, function and decoration, and a union of art and craft.

It became clear to me that between them the Arts and Crafts designers had cast an enormous stone into the stagnant waters of Victorian design, whose waves of influence affect fabric and interior design even today.

Discovering stencilling

On my first visit to America, in 1970, I discovered the potential of stencilling as a decorative technique. I studied many examples of traditional Early American stencilling, which I loved for their naivety and charm. (Sadly, this simplicity has often been crudely translated, with the result that modern commercial stencils often seem clumsy to me.)

When I came back to England, I began using stencils to apply delicate yet flamboyant designs onto walls, ceilings, floors and furniture. I realized how useful stencilling is for visually softening hard edges and for bringing a room "together". Another of its attractions was its suitability for all styles of home, from a sophisticated city apartment to a simple country cottage.

Arts and Crafts designs

For design inspiration I quickly turned back to the Arts and Crafts designers, whose draughtsmanship I knew I could trust. I was fascinated by Philip Webb's lovely stencilled ceiling in the William Morris Room at the Victoria & Albert Museum. Although stencilling was not one of the principal crafts practised by the movement, many of the Arts and Crafts designers used it occasionally. Some, including Morris, had studied medieval stencilling techniques, and Morris had himself stencilled a ceiling at the Red House, his home in Kent.

I discovered that many other Arts and Crafts designs, for everything from tiles to textiles, could also be adapted for stencilling. The strong, flowing lines of these designs were very suitable for the stencils I wished to create – especially Morris's *Willow Bough* and *Daisy* designs, de Morgan's tiles and Burges's furniture. Soon I was incorporating them into everything from shop fronts to drawing-room friezes and bedroom fabrics.

Morris, in particular, had a real genius for flat, two-dimensional pattern, which is one reason his wonderfully

ABOVE

The red and indigo that I used for the garden bench project (page 112) are the two colourways in which the Brother Rabbit *fabric (see opposite) was originally printed.*

natural-looking yet stylized patterns are more popular than ever. Although many of the designs are intricate or even ornate, they are never fussy.

Seeking inspiration

Morris spent much of his time at the South Kensington Museum (now the Victoria & Albert Museum), gathering inspiration from medieval illuminated manuscripts, Spanish velvets, Turkish tiles and so on. Although he believed that design had begun to deteriorate after the Middle Ages, he was nevertheless strongly influenced by Italian woven textiles of the fifteenth, sixteenth and seventeenth centuries and by Persian and Turkish patterns. A number of other Arts and Crafts designers were also influenced by Persian, Islamic and, especially, medieval designs. Perhaps this wide range of sources from which the movement took inspiration is what gives their work its timeless appeal.

However, it was nature, most of all, that was Morris's sourcebook – not the exotic hothouse plants so popular at the time, but the birds and plants he observed closely in his own garden. He advised: "And for your teachers, let them be nature and history." Although his patterns had a formal framework, the motifs were fundamentally natural, and there was a sense of spontaneous growth. "Even where a line ends," he said, "it should look as if it had plenty of capacity for more growth." This ability to create complex, beautifully balanced patterns from natural forms without sacrificing any of their naturalism is for me the greatest attraction of Morris's work.

Subtle but vibrant colour

I also particularly like Morris's sophisticated and imaginative use of colour. To our eyes today, however, Arts and Crafts colours may seem a little dingy, so for my stencils I like to keep those subtle tones, but add a vibrancy by using

BELOW

The Arts and Crafts palette comprised many shades that I use in my own stencil designs, including lovely shades of green and blue as well as russets, warm browns, soft yellows and cream.

RIGHT
*This red lustre tile by William de Morgan
illustrates the distinctive rusty-red colour
and iridescent metallic surface of lustreware.
De Morgan, who revived this ancient
technique, undertook many commissions for
Morris's company. His tiles were the ceramic
counterpart of Morris's fabrics
and wallpapers.*

a rich background colour – for example, a deep red with blues and greens on top. I always think it's better to go for strong, clear hues than to be timid about colour.

Morris went to extraordinary lengths to get exactly the colours he wanted for his woven and printed textiles, studying ancient dyeing methods and the art of using natural dyes. Working with Thomas Wardle, the most skilful British dyer of the time, Morris used a range of natural pigments – indigo and woad for blues; madder, cochineal and kermes (sent from Greece) for reds; weld (from wild mignonette) for yellow; and walnut shells and roots for deep brown – which he combined like primary colours to create subtle but glowing colours.

Colour choice

Today, it is easier than ever to recreate the subtle palette of Morris and the other Arts and Crafts designers without having to resort to digging up roots or pulverizing insects. In Morris's time, the newly invented man-made dyes were harsh and overpowering, whereas modern technology allows extraordinary subtlety. A growing interest in historical authenticity and an appreciation of the colours and styles of other cultures have made our palettes more subtle and at the same time more daring. Paint manufacturers, responding to the more discriminating market, today offer a vast range of shades.

We now have the best of both worlds – the old and the new – at our fingertips. We can precisely recreate the Arts and Crafts colours to obtain just the right feeling in a room, or go for a totally different look, such as a bright and sunny Mediterranean palette. The situation in which the stencil is being used can be allowed to dictate the palette. William Morris might have been startled at the range of colours available to us today, but he would undoubtedly have produced some brilliantly innovative effects.

In this book the colours I have used to mix each shade are listed with the projects. The proportions, however, are up to you. You will have to experiment to achieve the colours shown in the photographs – and in many cases you will probably discover shades you prefer to mine.

You can, of course, use completely different colour combinations to suit your taste, decor or the item or surface you are stencilling. In fact, you should always aim to bring some of yourself into your stencilling. This is what I have done in adapting Arts and Crafts designs, and it was one of Morris's central tenets. He sought inspiration in the past, particularly beautiful textiles, but he did not intend just to copy the designs – he wanted to bring some of the spirit of the past into the present and future. He wrote, "Let us study it wisely, be taught by it, kindled by it; all the while determining not to imitate or repeat it; to have either no art at all, or an art which we have made our own."

Adapting Arts and Crafts designs

As a starting point for stencil designing, the Arts and Crafts movement offers a wealth of ideas to choose from. Very few of the movement's designers confined themselves to just one medium or surface; most moved easily from stained glass or illustration to fabrics, carpets or ceramics. This is probably one reason their designs can be adapted so easily to stencilling.

After you have tried some of the projects in this book and learned how to tailor them to your own requirements, you will probably want to seek out other Arts and Crafts designs to use as a basis for projects of your own. Adapting someone else's design is the quickest way to set the creative process in motion, and you needn't feel apologetic about it: you will be continuing a tradition as long as the history of design itself.

Many of the Arts and Crafts designers used particular motifs, such as the curling acanthus leaf (used in the Voysey carpet shown on page 13) and the daisy, time and again. Morris found the daisy motif in a medieval manuscript and used it on an early wallpaper design. His wife, Janey, embroidered it onto a hanging, which I have adapted for the wall hanging in the book (see page 50). It appears on William de Morgan's tiles and also many times in Walter Crane's illustrations and wallpapers. I have taken one example of a Crane daisy (page 11) and incorporated it in the

ABOVE

The café curtain stencil (see page 72) was inspired by the de Morgan red lustre tile shown opposite. Although both the materials and the colourways of the tile and curtain are dramatically different, the patterns are very similar. Sometimes designs require very little adaptation even when being used in a completely different way.

Lily & Daisy Screen (page 54). By using it on another surface, and drawing it in a slightly different way, it creates quite a different impression.

The willow bough motif is another motif that flowed through Morris's work, into Crane's illustrations and onto de Morgan's tiles and pots. The graceful willow tree lends itself well to intertwining designs full of movement. In rooms papered with Morris's *Willow Bough* wallpaper, such as the bedroom in the photograph below, the two tones in the colourway give it a lovely flowing rhythm, like the willow tree itself. On the coffee table based on this wallpaper (page 42), I've made the willow the centre of attention just as it is in Morris's design.

The spirit of the original

When looking for designs to use, find one that is simple yet strong – perhaps a portion of a carpet border, a wallpaper or a piece of furniture. Ask yourself whether you want a repeat pattern, whether you want it to flow freely or whether one motif will look right on its own. If you are using a natural form as the basis for the design, make use of tendrils and leaves to add movement and interest to the design. Once you have traced the design, you can then simplify it by cutting out fiddly detail, refining it and emphasizing the main structural lines, until you have a good working design.

There is no need to use an entire design. Sometimes the design is too complicated to transfer in its entirety onto a stencil. Analyse what it is that you like – the colour, the spacings, just one motif or whatever – and use that element alone. You can have a lot of fun with this free approach and still retain the spirit of the original.

I particularly liked the border of a Morris carpet, which I incorporated in the Daisy Design Wall Hanging (page 50), copying the random colours. Similarly, the stencilled porcupine from William Burges's beautifully decorative cabinet is too good just to leave there. I imagined it running along a skirting (baseboard) or the bottom of a

ABOVE AND LEFT
The trailing willow bough was one of William Morris's favourite motifs, and Willow Bough, which was used for wallpaper and fabric, was probably his best-known design. The shape and colours make the motif ideal for an all-over stencilled pattern, as on the coffee table project (page 42).

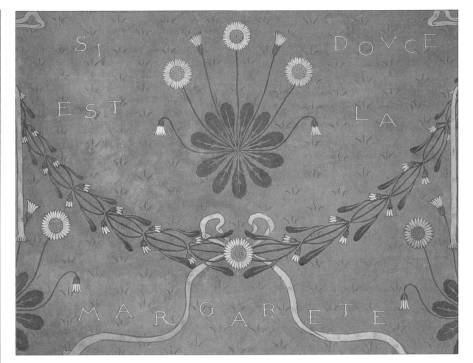

LEFT AND BELOW
The daisy was widely used in Arts and Crafts designs. The one shown on the left is from a Walter Crane wallpaper, La Margarete, *printed in 1875-6; the stencilled daisy in the screen project (page 54) was derived from this. Crane based his daisy on Morris's, and the latter was also the inspiration for the stencilled daisy shown below, which comes from the wall hanging project (page 50).*

window blind (shade) – in the event, I used it along the edge of a garden bench (page 112).

If you find a stencil you like but it is too large for the surface you want to use it on, it is perfectly feasible to change the scale, although you should make sure that the proportions are right for the room and for the surface you are stencilling. For example, the design for the pelmet, window seat and wallpaper border (see page 36 and overleaf) came originally from a small border surrounding some music in Walter Crane's songbook *Pan Pipes* (also shown overleaf); its size was increased three- or four-fold.

Another example is the de Morgan red lustre tile shown on page 8, which inspired the café curtain project on page 72. What attracted me to this design was its timelessness. I liked its soft, wind-blown look, and the proportions were good, so I felt it was possible to enlarge it and to paint it on a completely different surface in colours to suit my room, without losing the original spirit. Similarly, for the tile design on page 76, I enlarged Philip Webb's tiny swan and sprig motifs to use as individual "tiles"; in the original, sixteen of these motifs appeared on one tile.

Unlimited options

Part of the pleasure of using Arts and Crafts designs as a source of inspiration stems from the challenge of re-using a design in what may be a dramatically different way. While the bed cover, wall hanging, floral wall, cushion and floor-cloth projects in this book are similar to the items from which the designs were taken, other projects emphatically are not. The design for the wooden planter, for example, came from a stained glass window, and the motif for the garden trug was taken from a carpet border. The director's chair stencil was inspired by a tile, the bath panelling was

based on a sideboard, and the dining table came from a woodcut border. The design is what matters, not the source. Free yourself of any inhibitions about this and you will find the creative process much easier. If a design is good it can take on many forms and still look right.

The easiest approach is first to decide *what* you want to stencil, and look at it in its surroundings. Next, find a design that is the right proportion and weight for the space. Finally, choose the colours. When the stencilling is finished, it should look like part of the object, rather than superfluous decoration.

ABOVE AND RIGHT

The soft colours and flowing lines of a delicate Walter Crane border provided the inspiration for the stencil pattern on the right. The border surrounded one of Crane's illustrations (shown above) in Pan Pipes, *a book of old songs published in 1883. For the Jasmine Border Design (page 36), the tiny motif has been enlarged and used on a wallpaper border, window seat and pelmet (cornice).*

Using a sketch-book

I like to start off my stencils in a sketch-book, drawing them up into workable designs (see pages 26–7 for how to do this yourself), and also sometimes drawing how I think they will look once they are stencilled on the wall, furniture or whatever. In addition, the sketch-book is a good place to write down any notes, measurements and other relevant points and to play with different colourways. Some of my experiments for the Swan & Sprig Tile Pattern project are shown in the photograph of my sketch-book opposite.

In the same photograph you can see my designs for the floorcloth on page 98. This was based on a carpet by Voysey, one of the most important designers of the time. Here I remained faithful to the original carpet (also shown opposite), from which I took both the design and the strong colours. I then used small elements from the floorcloth to decorate the accompanying bathroom cabinet, keeping it in the same style but simplifying it with one repeated pattern.

The ornate pattern of the Voysey carpet is typical of many Arts and Crafts patterns. Yet many others – including another Voysey design, *Green Pastures*, which I used for the garden trug on page 117 – are notable for their simplicity. The Arts and Crafts designers didn't see this as a contradiction, since both approaches sprang from the integrity of the craftsman–artist.

I like the challenge of an ornate design, combining a geometric border with a more lifelike motif in the centre, such as on the dresser project on page 62. On the other hand, there is no substitute for the satisfaction of using one simple design in exactly the right place.

Incorporating stencils into your house

In designing the interiors of their own homes and those of their clients, William Morris and his colleagues aimed to create a whole look rather than just isolated elements. The principle applies equally to stencilling today. Stencilled decoration should enhance without looking superfluous. Dotting stencils around the room in a piecemeal fashion can only distract. Plan the stencil's use carefully. Make it exactly the shape you need, and relate the colours to those

RIGHT AND BELOW
My sketch-books contain the designs, measurements, sketches and experimental colourways for all the projects in this book. The photograph on the right shows my preliminary work on the tile project (page 76) and the floorcloth and bathroom cabinet project (page 98). The floorcloth was based on the Voysey carpet shown below; this is another example of a design that I changed very little.

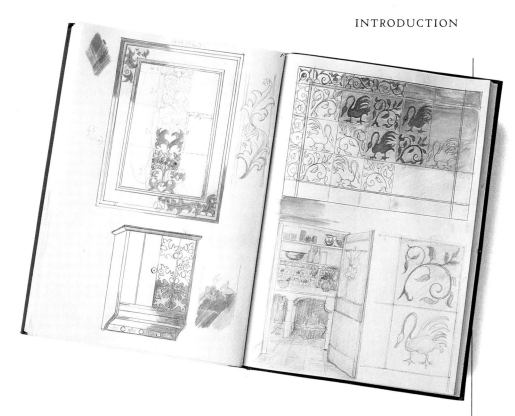

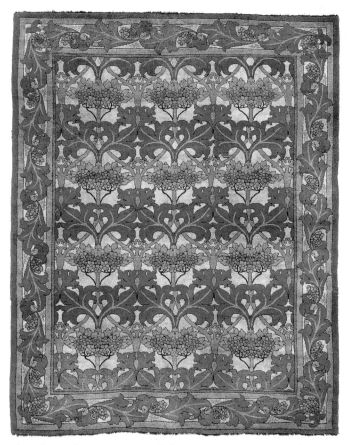

was, as Morris explained, "to restore the dignity of art to ordinary household decoration". His famous dictum, "Have nothing in your house which you do not know to be useful or believe to be beautiful," sums up his approach to decorating and furnishing a home. To Morris and his fellow Arts and Crafts designers, beautiful surroundings were essential for improving the quality of life.

Understanding the material

Morris and his colleagues believed that craftsmen had one huge advantage over designers who did not execute their own designs: firsthand experience of the possibilities and limitations of the material. Morris had an instinctive understanding of a material's potential, but he also strongly recommended getting your hands dirty. (For Morris, this was literally the case: during the years when he was striving to achieve the perfect indigo dye, his hands were almost permanently blue, causing his friends much amusement.) "The special limitations of the material," he advised, "should be a pleasure to you, not a hindrance." This applies not only to the plaster, wood, paper or fabric that you are stencilling but also to the paint and stencils.

After watching Morris creating a design, the Arts and Crafts architect W R Lethaby explained the process: "The forms . . . were *stroked* into place, with a sensation like that of stroking a cat . . . It was to express this sensuous pleasure that he used to say that all good designing was felt in the stomach."

Morris and his Arts and Crafts colleagues recognized the pleasure and satisfaction that hand crafting provides, whether it is weaving, stained-glass work or stencilling. I hope that this book will help you to discover the same pleasure in stencilling that I have found.

already in the room. Avoid the temptation to stencil everything in sight – your work will have much more impact if you use the stencil boldly but sparingly.

Follow the example of the Arts and Crafts designers, with their emphasis on strong, unfussy pattern. Their aim

Tools & Materials

Brushes: Seek out good-quality *stencil brushes* that feel soft, not stiff or hard. (I sometimes make my own by cutting off the tip of a round sash brush.) Many jobs will require four to six brushes, because you need one for each colour family that you are using as well as various sizes. You will also need a fine *artist's brush* or a special *lining brush* for touching up and detailing, one or two *decorator's brushes* for painting backgrounds, and a *varnishing brush*. (A *sponge* can be used instead of a brush for stencilling or for creating a textured background – see page 22.)

Paints: Most projects in this book use *acrylic paints*, which are water-based. They dry quickly, are very hard and waterproof when dry and can be mixed with other water-based paints, like *emulsion (latex)*. They are used straight from the tube (see page 20). Colours you will need most often are raw umber, raw sienna, crimson, Payne's grey and white. Other colours frequently used in the projects are Naples yellow, red oxide, Hooker's green, ultramarine, cobalt blue and cerulean blue. *Emulsions* and *historic-colour paints* can be used for stencilling large, simple patterns; buy sample pots for small amounts. *Fabric paints* can be used on fabrics (see page 16). *Signwriter's paints* (*Japan* or *bulletin colors*), which are oil-based, are excellent for outdoor projects, as they are quick-drying and hard. They are available from specialist suppliers. Stencilling can also be done with *spray paints*, but I do not enjoy working with them and they are not used in this book. *Artist's oil paints* are not suitable for stencilling as they take a long time to dry and are sticky.

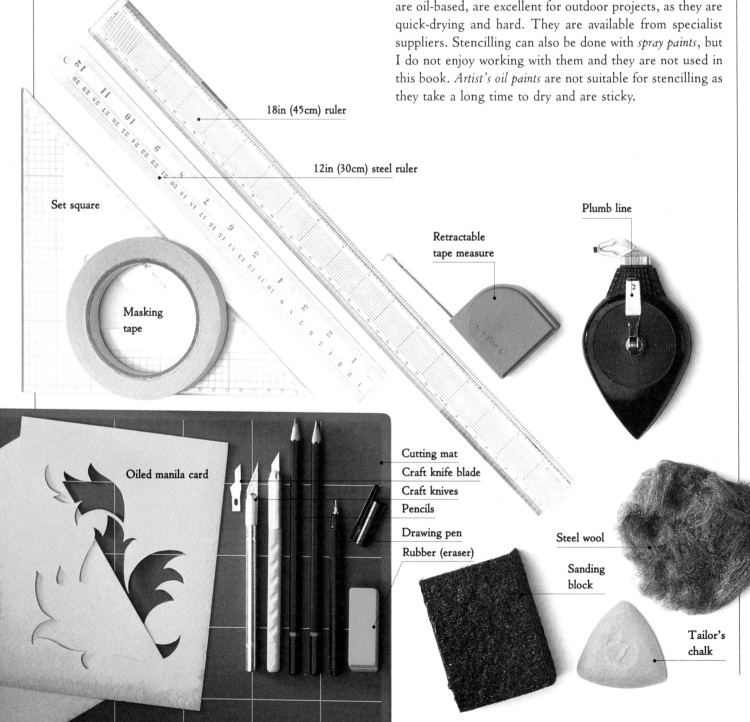

Set square

18in (45cm) ruler

12in (30cm) steel ruler

Masking tape

Retractable tape measure

Plumb line

Oiled manila card

Cutting mat
Craft knife blade
Craft knives
Pencils
Drawing pen
Rubber (eraser)

Steel wool

Sanding block

Tailor's chalk

Mediums: Many of the projects in this book call for *acrylic medium* or *fabric medium*. Adding a drop or two to your paint on the palette will make it more flexible and translucent without actually making it runnier. On fabrics it will help prevent the paint from chipping. If you are stencilling in hot weather and are using acrylic paints that are drying out too quickly, a little *acrylic retarding medium* can be added to slow the process down slightly.

Stencils: I cut stencils from *oiled manila card*, which doesn't slip, is easy to draw on and cut out and is long-lasting. *Acetate* is the main alternative. It is see-through, which is useful when tracing a design and also when stencilling (until the paint builds up). It is long-lasting but tricky to cut.

Other tools and materials: Put paints on a *paper plate* with a *palette knife*. Draw stencils with a *drawing pen* or *pencils* and a fine *felt-tipped pen*. Use a *pencil* for marking most surfaces, but *tailor's chalk* for fabrics. (To remove, brush it off with a clean brush.) For cutting stencils use a sharp *craft knife*. A *cutting mat* is useful, or use thick cardboard. To measure and mark walls, you need a retractable steel *tape measure*, *spirit level* (carpenter's level) and *plumb line*. For drawing lines and measuring other surfaces you will need *rulers*. A *set square* is useful for making square corners, but you can make your own from stiff card. Use low-tack *masking tape* to mask out unwanted portions of the stencil and hold it in place while stencilling. "Low-tack" means that there is less risk of its pulling off part of the surface.

Signwriter's paint

Fabric paints

Artist's brushes

Lining brush

Small stencil brushes

Medium stencil brush

Large stencil brush

Decorator's brushes

Acrylic paint

Large, stubby stencil brush

Sponge

Palette knife

Surfaces

The projects in this book involve stencilling on wood, plaster, fabric and paper, all of which are relatively easy to stencil. Non-absorbent surfaces like tiles, glazed pottery, enamelware and glass are difficult to decorate because the paint adheres badly and will wear off easily.

Preparation: The surface must be clean, smooth and free of wax or oil-based varnish. If it is painted, the paint should ideally be a fairly flat finish, although by sanding down with fine steel wool and taking a little extra care when stencilling, you can stencil on a slightly shiny surface. Choose emulsion (latex) or vinyl silk (latex velvet), both of which are water-based and generally used for walls, or eggshell, which is oil-based and used for woodwork.

Colourwashing: The softly dappled texture of a colourwash makes a good background for a stencil design on walls and on wood such as pine.

Sealing: After painting a wood surface with emulsion paint but before stencilling it, it is usually a good idea to seal the surface with flat emulsion (latex) glaze, which is a weak, water-based varnish.

Varnishing: After stencilling, any hard surfaces that will be washed or will be subject to wear should be sealed. For water-based paints, use an acrylic varnish or polyurethane. Polyurethane is more hard-wearing but is slow-drying and yellows with age, while acrylic varnish is less hard-wearing but is fast-drying and does not yellow. Both come in various finishes, from flat to gloss.

Fabrics: When stencilling onto fabric, protect your work surface from paint, and make the fabric as flat and taut as possible, taping down the edges. Use acrylics mixed with fabric medium (see page 15) or fabric paints. To make stencilled fabric hand-washable, "fix" fabric paints with a hot iron, following the manufacturer's instructions.

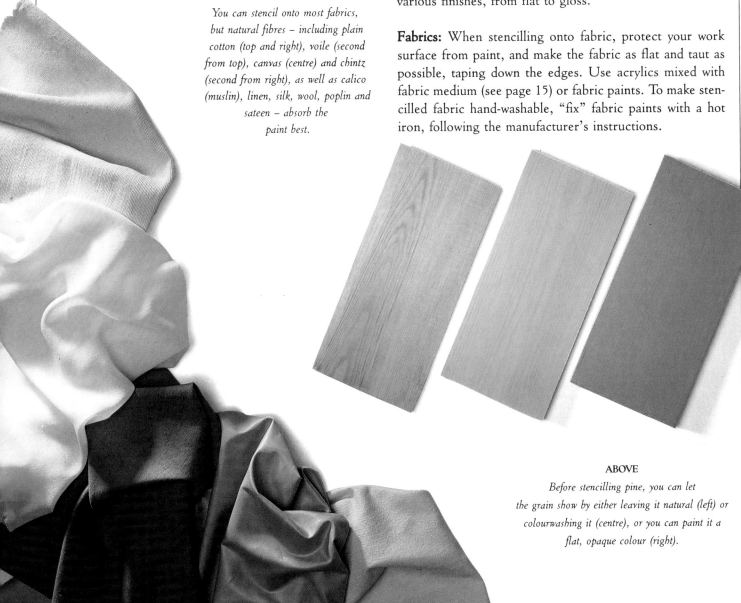

BELOW

You can stencil onto most fabrics, but natural fibres – including plain cotton (top and right), voile (second from top), canvas (centre) and chintz (second from right), as well as calico (muslin), linen, silk, wool, poplin and sateen – absorb the paint best.

ABOVE

Before stencilling pine, you can let the grain show by either leaving it natural (left) or colourwashing it (centre), or you can paint it a flat, opaque colour (right).

LEFT

Varnish not only protects a surface, it also brings out the stencil colours. Use a varnishing brush to apply it, and try to avoid dust. Apply one or more thin coats, allowing it to dry between applications. Sand lightly with fine sandpaper or steel wool between coats.

LEFT

Think about the colours and textures that will form a background to your stencilling. While some colours will enhance each other, others will just clash. Similarly, a "broken" finish like the colourwash on this wall can often complement a stencilled design perfectly. To colourwash a wall, first apply a base coat of emulsion (latex) in white or a pale colour, criss-crossing the brush strokes. When dry, dilute a toning shade of emulsion, such as pale yellow or blue, with water. Brush on two coats in the same criss-cross manner. If you prefer, use a sponge instead of a brush to apply this.

Cutting a Stencil

If your stencil template is the correct size, all you have to do is trace it and then transfer the image to stencil card. If you are making a stencil from acetate, you can trace the design straight onto the acetate using a permanent marker.

Enlarging: The templates in this book have had to be reduced to 40 per cent, 50 per cent or 60 per cent of the original size. If you want to use them at the original size, they will need to be enlarged to 250 per cent, 200 per cent and 167 per cent respectively. This information is given with the templates for each project. All the templates for any one project have been reduced by the same amount.

Using a photocopier: The simplest way to enlarge a template is on a photocopier. Unfortunately, brands of photocopiers vary in the way they do this. The safest approach is to measure one dimension on one stencil and then work out the new dimension yourself on a calculator simply by finding 250 per cent, 200 per cent or 167 per cent

HOW TO CUT A STENCIL

1 *Enlarge the stencil template to the correct size if necessary, then, using a very soft (6B) pencil, trace the outline of the stencil onto tracing paper. Remember that the finished stencil will actually be the mirror image of this.*

2 *Turn the tracing over and place it pencilled side down on the stencil card, leaving sufficient border all around. Tape the tracing to the card. Using a hard (H) or medium (HB) pencil, draw over the lines, pressing quite hard.*

ABOVE

The cut-out portions of stencils can sometimes be used themselves as stencils if you cut a design into them. Veins could be cut out of these leaf centres, for example, to stencil over the stencilled leaves in a different colour. In this book cut-out centres used in this way are shown separately for clarity, but are in fact cut out of the main stencil.

of the old dimension. Ask the photocopying bureau to enlarge it to that size, and to enlarge all the other stencils for that project by the same amount. For example, if a template in the book is 4in (10cm) long and needs to be enlarged to 250 per cent, it should measure 10in (25cm) after it has been photocopied.

Customizing a stencil: In many instances you will need to enlarge, or even reduce, a stencil by a different amount in order to fit different dimensions of, say, a wall, floor, fabric or piece of furniture. The procedure is much the same. Simply decide what the crucial dimension is on the stencil, and ask the photocopying bureau to enlarge or reduce the template enough to make it that size.

The grid method: If you don't have access to a photocopier that will do this, you can enlarge or reduce it manually. Draw a grid over the template. Measure out the desired finished size on a piece of paper and draw in a grid with the same number of squares. Now copy the design onto the new grid square by square.

Reverse image: The stencil will be the mirror image of the design you have traced. If it isn't symmetrical, and if you want it to be the same way around as the design, turn over the completed tracing and trace the lines on the back using a very soft pencil.

Large stencils: If your template is larger than the stencil card, join two pieces of card with masking tape on both sides, butting up the edges.

Margins: On the stencil, allow at least 2in (5cm) all around the edges of a design for strength and also to help prevent smudges. For some designs, making the margin a particular size will help in positioning repeats.

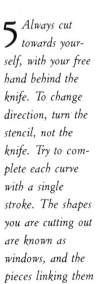

3 Remove the tape and peel the tracing away. The design will have transferred to the stencil card. It will probably be quite faint, so strengthen the lines if necessary by drawing over them.

4 Hold your craft knife in your right hand (or your left hand if you are left-handed) in an upright position. Use your other hand to hold the stencil card, but not too near the knife. Start cutting near the centre of the design.

5 Always cut towards yourself, with your free hand behind the knife. To change direction, turn the stencil, not the knife. Try to complete each curve with a single stroke. The shapes you are cutting out are known as windows, and the pieces linking them are called ties or bridges.

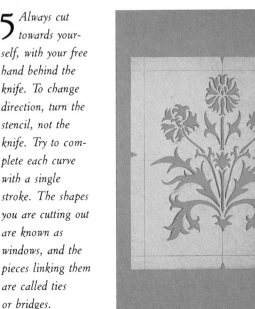

6 Transfer any registration marks (such as notches cut into the sides or small holes in the centre) which are on the template, or make your own if required. These are used to line up with a previous imprint to help in positioning.

Starting to Stencil

Masking: If a window in a stencil is so close to another that you might accidentally smudge the wrong colour through it, mask the window out using tape or a piece of card. Masking is not necessary if the two colours will be blended anyway, such as on a leaf that has dark and light sides.

Positioning the stencil: If you are stencilling a wall, decide if there is somewhere the stencil needs to be symmetrical, such as a chimney breast or on either side of a window or door, and then start at that point. The design should fit exactly at each corner of a wall, so make any adjustments in the spacing before you get to the corner, "stretching" or "shrinking" the design gradually and imperceptibly. When sticking a large, finely cut stencil on the wall, some people use non-permanent spray adhesive, but I find that masking tape is usually enough. Use tape to attach the stencil to wood and fabric, too. To help you reposition the stencil for each repeat, or to position another stencil over the first imprint, use registration marks, in the form of lines or cut-out notches or holes.

Mixing paint: Squeeze your paints from the tubes into a jar (such as a baby food jar or a miniature jam jar) and mix together. It is very easy to overdo it and get too dark a colour. Try to mix up enough paint for the entire job; store it with the lid on the jar. Gauging how much you need is always difficult but for the main colour of a frieze in an average-sized room, mix enough to fill a small glass jar. If you run short, mix some more before you've run out of the first so that you can match the colours. Compare wet paint against wet, as the colours change slightly when dry.

Taking up paint with the brush: You will need only the smallest amount of paint on the brush. If it is the right consistency – neither too wet nor too dry – the paint should slide off the brush, leaving a soft, even mark.

STENCILLING WITH A BRUSH

1 *One stencil may involve more than one colour. Where another colour is close to the one you are stencilling, mask that window or part of the window either with tape or by holding a piece of stencil card over it.*

2 *Mark where you'll want the stencil to go and position it carefully, using the registration marks to help you. Tape it in place at each corner. Be careful not to stencil through cut-out registration marks.*

LEFT
Whether you use a long stencil brush with a small head or a fat, stubby brush, there is no need for the paint to rise more than ¹/₄in (6mm) up the bristles.

3 *Mix up only small amounts of paint while you are adjusting the colour. When you are happy with the shade, mix up enough for the whole job. Put a little of the paint near the edge of a paper plate.*

Using the brush: Most people believe that stencilling has to be done with the dabbing action known as pouncing, but many stencillers use this only occasionally. Most of the time I use a looser, more swirling action, which gives the effect I want and is also quicker and less tiring. Pressing very gently, start at the edges of a window so that the colour will be softer at the centre. Concentrate on any small corners to make them crisp. When the windows are narrow, a circular motion is not possible, so move the brush back and forth, or use a dabbing action. You may have to press quite hard when the paint is almost gone from the brush.

Cleaning brushes: After stencilling, clean your brushes carefully. For acrylic or fabric paint, wash the brushes out well in warm (not hot) water until the water runs clean. If the paint is beginning to dry on the brush, use some washing-up liquid, working it in with your fingers. Rinse well and shake out excess water. For oil-based paints, use turpentine substitute before washing. If the brushes are not going to be needed for a while, wrap paper around the bristles to help them keep their shape. If you are using them straight away, dry them with a paper towel.

ABOVE

Pouncing – stippling on the colour by lightly bouncing the brush up and down – creates a less clear imprint. Different colours can be applied on top of each other with this technique.

BELOW

A firm, even, rhythmic circular motion with a soft brush produces a soft but clear image. This is the most effective method and is excellent for blending in different colours and shading.

4 *With a barely damp brush, take up a very tiny amount of paint. Work the paint into the brush on the plate, using a circular motion, then test the consistency on paper before starting to stencil.*

5 *Hold the brush like a pen, but upright, so the ends of the bristles are flat on the surface. Stencil, pressing only lightly at first. Use a circular, swirling action or, occasionally, a dabbing action known as pouncing.*

21

Special Effects

Use a variety of techniques to make your stencilling more interesting. Combining two colours within one shape looks lovely if you avoid any hard edges. To create a three-dimensional effect, make the centre lighter and the edges darker, by either fading away the colour till it disappears in the centre, darkening it around the edges or using a deeper colour to shade the edges and a lighter one for highlights. The effect should be subtle.

As an alternative to hand-painting details, cut a design (such as a flower centre or leaf veins) out of a piece you have removed when cutting the stencil, then use it after the main stencil.

When stencilling with a sponge, dab a little paint on the sponge, rolling it around to coat it evenly, then lightly pounce it through the stencil. Do not overdo it or you will lose the sponge pattern.

To hand-paint a fine line, fill up your brush with a fairly wet paint and pull it along a pencilled guide line, moving your whole arm and even your body. If necessary, touch up with the background colour.

When you are stencilling right up against a skirting (baseboard), ceiling or window sill, fold the edge of the stencil to the front so that it will fit into the angle and also protect the surface. For a small, cramped area, make a small stencil just for the relevant portion of the design.

STENCILLING EDGES ONLY
*Lightly stencilling just around the edges
of a shape often creates a feeling
of movement.*

STENCILLING WITH A SPONGE
*A sponge can be used for large, simple
prints. Coarse sponges (top) and fine-textured
ones (bottom) create different
imprints. A natural sponge creates an
interesting texture but a man-made one can be
used if torn into an uneven shape.*

BLENDING COLOURS
*To blend the edges of two colours used
in one shape, brush them lightly together
in the middle.*

SHADING

One way to add a feeling of depth is to deepen the colour around the edge by using your brush more heavily.

HIGHLIGHTING

Another way to create depth is to use a different, slightly lighter colour in the centre from the colour used around the edges.

CUT-OUT CENTRES

For leaf veins, use a cut-out centre from the main leaf to create a separate stencil.

PAINTING STRIPES

Stencilled stripes

are easy to stencil if the stencil is no longer than about 12in (30cm). Do not paint right to the end. Instead, soften the end by fading away the colour. Now move the stencil along so that it overlaps the painted area, and continue stencilling, softening this end too.

Stripes using tape

Another way to paint stripes is with two rows of tape the same distance apart as the desired width of the stripe. Stick the tape down firmly on the inner edge. Paint right up to the tape, then, when the paint is completely dry, pull the tape off gently, bending it back on itself.

Hand-painted stripes

To hand-paint a fine line with an artist's brush or a lining brush, you can steady your hand as you paint by running your little finger along a ruler. The more relaxed and comfortable you are, the easier it is.

Trouble-Shooting

Even the most experienced stencillers make mistakes, but some of the commonest problems can be prevented very easily, while others can be rectified without too much trouble. Moreover, one of the attractions of stencilling is that many so-called mistakes can be regarded as individual features rather than errors.

Unevenness: If you are stencilling around a room, you will find that you get into a rhythm of working, taking up paint on your brush at fairly regular intervals. The gradual softening of the colour that occurs as the paint diminishes each time, means that your working rhythm translates into a

visual rhythm in the stencilling. Don't feel that you should try to make the paint consistent all around – this rhythm is part of its charm. Similarly, don't worry about individual places that are uneven, or about tiny splatters. They simply emphasize the fact that this is hand-painting, thereby adding variety and interest to the design.

Touching up: If you do need to touch up some stencilling at the end, perhaps along a straight line that has suddenly wobbled, a small brush and the background paint you used can work wonders. Try to keep some of the paint for precisely this purpose.

COMMON MISTAKES

Powdery look
If your stencilling looks powdery and the paint doesn't move off the brush, the acrylic paint or the brush is too dry. Add a little acrylic medium, or one drop of water, to the paint on your palette, and mix them with your palette knife.

Heavy effect
A common mistake is to take too much paint onto the brush. Even when the paint consistency is right, using too much paint will make the stencilling look heavy and crude. Start again, and this time take only the tiniest amount.

Fuzzy edges
If your brush is too wet, it will make the paint too wet, causing it to bleed under the stencil, which gives fuzzy edges. Mix up more paint, dry your brush on a paper towel so it is just damp and then start again. To test whether it is too damp, squeeze the tip – it should not froth up.

Smudges
A speck of paint on the back of the stencil will cause a smudge, so check the back often. If you do get a smudge wipe it off immediately or wait until it is dry then paint over it with the background paint and a small brush.

Smudges on fabric: Fabrics are less forgiving than hard surfaces, as they are so absorbent. Correcting mistakes is virtually impossible on fabric, although occasionally you can scratch a stray blob of paint off after it has dried. The secret of success in stencilling fabric is to follow the advice on page 16 – and take care.

Care of stencils: Taking good care of your stencils will help prevent problems too. Strengthen any stencils that are very delicate by applying a coat of flat acrylic varnish to both sides of the card. Do not allow paint to build up on the stencils – clean it off as you go. To stop stencils from getting bent or otherwise damaged, let them dry thoroughly for at least a day after use, and then store them flat in a cool, dry place. Ideally, put sheets of cardboard between the layers and place the stencils on shelves.

BELOW
Acrylic paints are generally the right consistency straight from the tube; diluting them will make them too runny. Even a brush that is too wet can have this effect, so make sure your brush is only just damp.

Torn tie
If a tie gets torn when you are cutting a stencil or while you are stencilling, repair it with masking tape. Just patch each side of the stencil with a tiny piece of tape which is the same width as the torn tie.

Rough edges
A badly cut stencil will give your work a rough outline. Hold the stencil up to the light and check for rough edges, then cut off any ragged pieces. Replace the blade on your craft knife often so it is always sharp.

Designing Stencils

ABOVE
To make a stencil from flowers, you need to eliminate superfluous details.

Once you have some stencilling experience and have become familiar with how the elements of a set of stencils interrelate, you may wish to design your own stencils. Initially, it is easier to start with an existing pattern. Fabrics and carpets are good sources for designs, especially if you want to, say, copy your curtains or bed cover and turn the design into a frieze around the room, or echo a motif on an old kilim rug in a floor border.

If you want to design a stencil that is not a pattern but something more representational, you could trace a picture from a book or magazine, since the image has already been reduced from three dimensions to two. A stylized design or architectural drawing is easier to turn into a stencil than a realistic image or photograph, but all are possibilities and worth experimenting with.

DESIGNING FROM NATURE

1 *Choose some flowers as a starting point. Look at them closely. Find where the natural breaks and joins are – where the leaves join the stem, or a flower stalk branches off. Note the shapes of buds and the sizes of flowers. Now make a colour drawing of the flowers.*

2 *Simplify your drawing by tracing it, leaving out unnecessary leaves and emphasizing other parts. Plan where the ties should go and try out different colourways. Now trace this design, drawing only the basic outline of each of the shapes.*

3 *Move the tracing to the top of the design and see how the repeat will look. Try using the reverse side. Add extra leaves or petals to fill any awkward gaps. Redraw portions of it if necessary. Finally, retrace the whole design, including the repeats.*

4 *Transfer your design from the tracing paper to a piece of stencil card and cut it out, as directed on page 19.*

Alternatively, start from nature and try your hand at drawing it yourself. It is best to choose something that is not too difficult to draw.

After you have completed the basic drawing, the next stage is to simplify it down into its basic qualities or underlying structure. In creating a stencil, you are breaking the image down into separate shapes held together by ties. The ties are absolutely crucial to the design. They hold the stencil together, both physically and visually.

To be functional, ties need to be about $^{1}/_{8}$in (3mm) wide, and about 3–4in (7.5–10cm) apart, but their exact size, shape and position depend on the design. For example, you wouldn't add a hard line in the form of a tie across a stem. Ties should follow the lines of the design and appear at natural points in it, so that they are not noticeable. They can be short or long, and straight, slanted or curved to match the surrounding shapes. In an area where the windows are large, the ties may look better large too. Similarly, where the windows are small and intricate, the ties can be delicate.

ABOVE

Tracing a design from a patterned textile is not difficult. If the pattern is symmetrical, you need only trace half of it, as the tracing can be turned over to create the mirror image.

ADAPTING A TEXTILE PATTERN

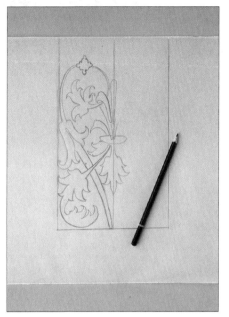

1 *To take a design from fabric or a carpet, lay it out on a hard surface. Pin or tape tracing paper over it and trace around the design with a very soft pencil. Transfer the tracing onto paper by placing it face down and drawing over the lines, pressing hard.*

2 *On the paper, work out your colourways and which colours will go on each stencil. It is a good idea to keep the colours separate – for example, red and blue on one stencil, and green and yellow on another. You also need to decide at this stage the position of the ties.*

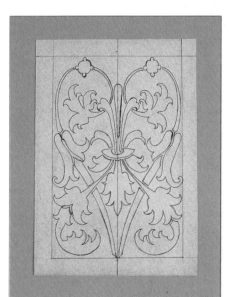

3 *Retrace the elements of the design relating to one stencil, and transfer it to stencil card. Repeat for each stencil you are using. Make a registration mark appropriate to the design.*

HALLS &
LIVING ROOMS

A hall gives visitors their first impression of a home, but a typical hall has lots of doors and very little wall space. A stencil design for the floor, such as the dramatic one overleaf, offers perhaps the most scope here. Other possibilities include running a frieze around the walls above the picture rail (if any) and doorways, which would help to unify the room, or stencilling the door surrounds or doors themselves. If there is a stairway, a border running up the wall alongside it could look good. Using the same stencil in both the hall and an adjacent room, such as the living room, will help to link the two rooms visually.

In a living room there is infinite scope for stencilling, and you will find a wide variety of living room projects in this chapter, for walls, furniture and soft furnishings.

Fuchsia & Leaf Floor Design

Taken from the border of a carpet designed by William Morris, this stencil design is ideal for floors. Not only is it infinitely adaptable, but the large scale enables quick progress to be made, even when stencilling a good-sized floor.

ABOVE AND OPPOSITE
Brownish-black paint is used for most of this stencil design and looks dramatic against natural wood floorboards. Tiny fuchsia flowers in deep cherry red add a little colour without diluting the impact of the sooty black stencilling.

This wide border pattern comes from one of William Morris's Hammersmith carpets (which was what his firm's hand-knotted rugs were called, because they were originally made in the coach house and stable at Morris's home in Hammersmith, west of London). Like embroidered hangings and tapestries, Hammersmith carpets were individual works of art, in contrast to the machine-woven carpets also produced by his firm.

To Morris, the border was at least as important as the centre of a carpet. He felt that it should incorporate more than one motif, stating that "all borders should be made up of several members, even where they are narrow, or they will look bald and poor, and ruin the whole cloth". He also often used the same border with different centres – either patterned or plain – and on both hand-knotted and machine-woven carpets. In the case of this border, the centre was plain and took up roughly the same proportion of the whole carpet as the unstencilled part of the floor in the photograph opposite.

This design is well suited to stencilling, as the pattern is strong and bold and can be adapted to different spaces and angles. In a narrow hall, it could go around the edges of the room, as here. In a wider room, the main motif from the border could be used twice, end to end, as a medallion in the centre of the floor.

You will find with this stencil that you can cover a lot of floor quite quickly, but it is important to take care over the corners. The edges of the mitre need to be really sharp and even, so avoid stencilling too far into the corner at once – it's better to stencil too little and have to go back and do a bit more than to go too far.

When the whole floor is stencilled and the paint is dry, apply at least three coats of flat varnish. If desired, you can use floor polish to give it a nice sheen.

MATERIALS
Flat polyurethane or acrylic varnish
Acrylic paints:
Brownish-black: ivory black, burnt umber
Cherry red: crimson, Payne's grey

1 *Measure the floor along each wall, and mark the centre. Plan the design, marking the inner and outer edges of the border. Stencil the zigzag border in brownish-black all around the outer edge, softening the ends of the stripes (p 23, step 1).*

2 *Stencil the diamond border in brownish-black all around the inner edge of the design. As you reposition the stencil, line up the cut-out triangle at the end of the stencil with the leading diamond of those you have just stencilled.*

3 While the paint is still wet, move the stencil along a little so that you can stencil in the ties on the stripes, in order to make them continuous lines. (If you wait until they are dry, they will look uneven.)

4 The corners are mitred. On an outer corner, the lines that are nearest the corner should extend to their position after turning the corner. Stencil the stripes (but not the zigzags) up to this point.

5 Position the stencil around the corner, with the end lined up with the previous edge. Using a ruler as a guide, mask the stripes so that each will stop in line with where it has previously been stencilled. Stencil the stripes.

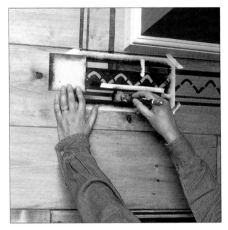

6 Put the stencil back on the previous edge, but further along so that you can stencil each stripe up to its counterpart on the other edge. Using masking tape or card, mask the ends of the stripes that you are stencilling.

7 Now stencil the zigzags on both sides of the corner. To make them meet at the mitre, you may need to move the stencil along slightly between repeats. Inner corners are done using the same technique in reverse.

8 Position the corner motif with the stems on the diagonal. Stencil the leaves and stems in brownish-black and the flowers in cherry red. Stencil the remaining border as steps 4–6. Stencil the diamonds last.

9 Position the main flower stencil between the inner and outer border. The number of times you repeat this motif, and the distance between the repeats, will depend upon the size of your room. However, it is important that the distance between each of these repeat flower motifs is the same.

10 Stencil all the leaves and stems in brownish-black, masking out nearby flowers if you wish. When the paint is dry, stencil the four flowers in cherry red, masking out adjacent leaves if necessary. When the paint is completely dry, paint on at least three coats of flat polyurethane or acrylic varnish.

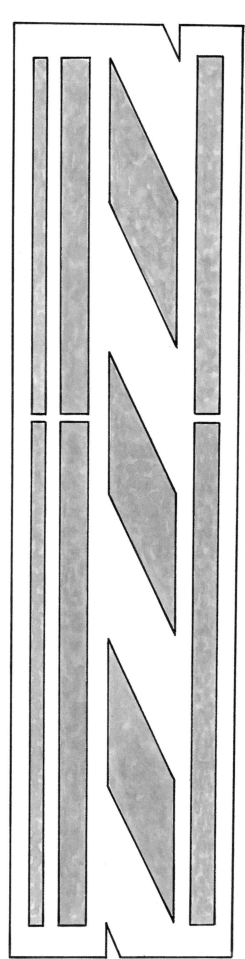

Diamond
border

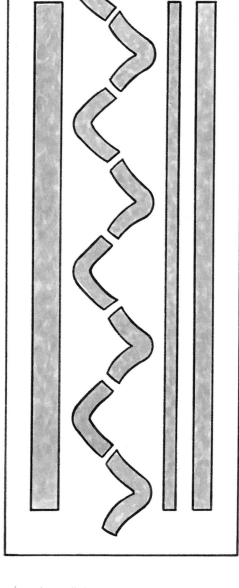

Zigzag
border

*Enlarge all the templates for this project to
200 per cent (see pages 18–19).*

*This border design consists of a large flower
stencil used at regular intervals
around the edge of the floor, with a different
flower stencil at the corners. A zigzag border
runs along the outer edge and a diamond
border along the inner edge.*

Large flower

Corner flower

Leaf Pattern Desk Set

This simple project was inspired by a small portion of a much more elaborate textile design by the influential Arts and Crafts designer Lindsay Butterfield. The stencils are extremely versatile and can be used on a variety of small items.

ABOVE
Elaborate colour schemes or sophisticated shading would be inappropriate for a simple design like this. The project is therefore ideal for beginners not only because of its small scale but also because the techniques involved are not advanced.

MATERIALS
Emulsion (latex) paint in dark indigo and red
Flat emulsion glaze
Flat acrylic varnish
Acrylic paints
Light blue: ultramarine, white,
a little raw umber

ABOVE AND OPPOSITE
In this writing set, the stencils have been arranged to fit the overall shape of each side of the letter rack and envelope box. Thus, the tallest element – the large leaf – is used in each case to emphasize the curved edge of the container.

The Lindsay Butterfield fabric *Canterbury Bells*, from which this leaf pattern is taken, was roller-printed by G P & J Baker in 1902. A prolific and highly successful designer, Butterfield created patterns for wallpapers as well as for woven and printed fabrics. He also produced a range of stencilled fabrics for the same company.

The simplest designs are often the most versatile, and the two small stencils used here are infinitely adaptable. The three elements of which they are comprised – a large leaf, a small leaf and a diamond – can be used together in various configurations or individually.

The box and letter rack are both painted with two coats of emulsion (latex) paint prior to stencilling. After painting but before stencilling, seal the surface with flat emulsion (latex) glaze. Finally, varnish with flat acrylic varnish when the stencilling has dried.

1 *Paint the box with blue emulsion (latex) on the outside and red on the inside. When dry, seal it with glaze. Use the large leaf stencil to stencil three leaves on one side of the box, starting with one at bottom centre, then to the left and right of it, near the top. INSET: Repeat on the other side, back and front, positioning the leaves further apart on the front and back than on the sides.*

Large leaf motif

Small leaf and diamond motif

2 *Now use the other stencil to add the small leaves and diamonds to the front and back of the box, at the bottom left, top centre and bottom right. If you prefer, or if the shape of the item dictates, use just a portion of the stencil, such as the small leaf, with only two diamonds, or even just the small leaf on its own.*

Enlarge both templates for this project to 167 per cent (see pages 18–19).

Just two stencils are used for both of these projects: a large leaf, and a small leaf surrounded by four diamonds. The same colour is used for both.

Jasmine Border Design

Based on a Walter Crane design, this border of jasmine flowers and foliage can be used on a pelmet (cornice) or wallpaper border and can be adapted for a wider area such as a window seat. Choose colours to suit your decor.

ABOVE AND OPPOSITE
The combination of a border design with randomly stencilled flowers and sprigs from the design not only makes this stencil versatile, but also adds visual interest. In a confined space like a window seat, the width of the border must be an exact fit.

This versatile border was inspired by a border around an illustration in *Pan Pipes*, an old book of songs illustrated by Walter Crane (see page 12). Crane's border is very illustrative and loose. The colours he used, which are similar to those used here, were pale olive green foliage with white jasmine flowers bearing yellow centres, on a warm apricot-coloured ground.

Here the border has been used not only on the pelmet (cornice) but also around the walls of the room. The height of the border on the walls was planned to correspond to the height of the top of the window seat, along which the border runs so that the line would be unbroken all the way around the room. However, if you don't have a window seat, the wallpaper border could just as well be used on its own, in which case you would probably wish to raise it to chair rail or picture rail height.

The wallpaper border is simplicity itself to stencil, and you can work in comfort on a flat surface before hanging it. Simply cut a strip of lining paper, being careful to make it straight and the same depth all the way along the strip – a metal straightedge and scalpel (mat knife) will work better than scissors for this. Place it on a flat surface, taping the edges, and then start stencilling at one end rather than in the centre as you do for the pelmet and window seat. When the paint is completely dry, hang it as you would normally, using heavy-duty wallpaper paste.

The outer green bands are not part of the stencil and so are painted beforehand, using masking tape to keep the lines straight. Be sure to use low-tack masking tape so that it is less likely to pull the paint off when you remove it. Use a 1in (2.5cm) flat decorator's brush to paint the lines. When stencilling the top edge of the window seat, you will not need to draw or mask the outer line, since the edge of the wood will provide enough of a guide line for painting straight.

MATERIALS
Eggshell paint in a terracotta shade
Flat polyurethane varnish
Acrylic paints:
Green: Hooker's green, raw sienna, white
Cream: White, a little raw sienna, a little raw umber
Yellow: Naples yellow

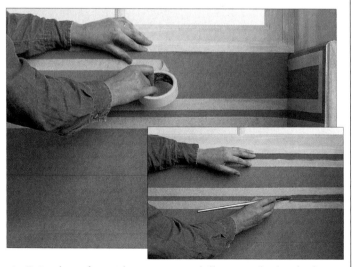

1 *Paint the surface with terracotta eggshell paint and rub it back with fine steel wool. Mark the edges of the stencil design and draw lines 1in (2.5cm) away from the edges. Run masking tape along these lines. INSET: Paint in the green band between the lines of tape.*

2 *Find the centre of the window seat back or the pelmet and the centre of the stencil. Position the stencil in the centre, taping it in place. (When you are working near the end of the window seat, you may need to fold the end of the stencil so that it will fit into the corner.) Mask off the flowers using tape.*

3 *Stencil the foliage in green. On a surface with a slight sheen, the stencilling can sometimes look patchy, so after the paint has dried you may need to go over it again using the same colour or a slightly lighter one. Now peel off the masking tape from the flowers, and stencil the flowers in cream.*

4 *With the stencil still in place, use the cut-out centre piece from each flower (each of which is different) to stencil on a yellow dot in the middle of the flower. You don't need to tape the cut-out piece in place – it can simply be held with the fingers. Use a very small stencil brush for this.*

5 *Lift off the stencil carefully, peeling it back from the stencilled surface, and clean off any paint if necessary. Now flip the stencil over and reposition it next to the stencilled area. Repeat the procedure. If the stencil does not fit into the space exactly, use a portion of it at the ends, bending the stencil gently.*

Enlarge both templates for this project to 167 per cent (see pages 18–19).

Border

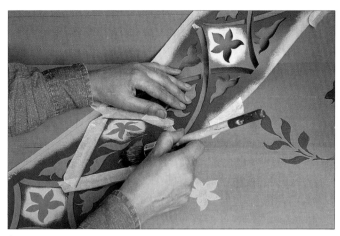

6 *For the vertical sides of the window seat, you will need to use only a portion of the border. Line up the centre of the stencil with the centre of the area to be stencilled. Bend the stencil around the outer corner and fold it at the inner corner, taping it securely in place. Now stencil as before.*

7 *The horizontal part of the window seat is stencilled only with random leaves and sprigs. Use the main stencil for this, masking out adjacent areas, such as the curved lines that run through the design, so that they will not get smudged with paint. Stencil some of these along the back, too. Finish with two coats of varnish.*

LEFT
Because you are cutting the wallpaper border yourself from lining paper, you can make it fit the depth of the stencil exactly, with the green bands butting right up to the edges.

One stencil is used to stencil the pelmet and wallpaper border and the top edge of the window seat. (The template for this should be joined at the dotted lines.) The flower centres are added using the cut-out centre from each one. Individual flowers and sprigs are stencilled onto the window seat using portions of the border stencil.

Central design for flower (cut one from each flower centre)

Willow Bough Coffee Table

This simplified version of William Morris's famous Willow Bough design makes an ideal overall pattern for a flat surface such as a coffee table. The colours used for the stencilling are much the same as those of the original wallpaper.

ABOVE AND OPPOSITE

The willow bough stencil design is made up of three sections, which fit together to create a flowing, intertwining pattern. It can be adapted to any flat surface, including not only the top of this table but also the table edge or even a small tray.

One of Morris's best-loved designs, *Willow Bough*, was the basis for this stencil design. Created in 1887 for wallpaper, it covered the walls of Morris's daughter May's bedroom. She found it delightful because of "the pleasant river scene it recalls".

Like the original, the design used here is suitable for most styles of decor because of its restful, undemanding, yet still interesting pattern.

Be sure to spend enough time planning your design before beginning to stencil. The rhythm of the pattern as it flows over the surface is important, and you will probably find that the figure-of-eight shape used here works best.

Because of the wear-and-tear most coffee tables are subjected to, it is important to protect the stencilling with varnish. Choose one with a flat finish. When it is dry, polish with furniture polish to give a soft sheen.

MATERIALS
White emulsion (latex) paint
Emulsion (latex) glaze
Flat acrylic varnish
Acrylic paints for background:
Soft brownish-pink: red oxide, a little white,
raw umber
Acrylic paints for stencilling:
Green: chromium oxide, a little cobalt blue
Yellow-green: chromium oxide, a little cobalt blue,
a little cadmium yellow
Reddish-brown: red oxide

1 *Plan where to position the repeats of the three stencils, drawing the design on tracing paper the same size as the tabletop. Remove the paper. Paint the table with a white undercoat followed by a thin colourwash of brownish-pink mixed with emulsion (latex) glaze to give an uneven background, brushing in the direction of the grain.*

2 *Stencil a thin green line (p 23) all around the tabletop, along the edge. Also stencil a thin green line along each vertical edge of the table legs. (You'll need to use a small brush for this and for the leaves in the remaining steps, and an even smaller brush for the leaf tips and stems in those steps.)*

3 *Lay the tracing paper on the tabletop. Start at one end and position the largest stencil underneath the tracing paper. Remove the tracing paper and stencil in the leaves in green, using a little yellow-green at the tips if you wish. Stencil the reddish-brown stems, fluffing the paint on only very lightly.*

4 *Again using the tracing paper as a guide, position the medium-sized stencil next, so it seems to grow out of the first one. Apply the green, yellow-green and reddish-brown paint to the leaves and stem as before.*

5 *Continue stencilling in this way, fitting the stencils together and using the small one to fill in. Turn them over sometimes. Use portions of the stencils to fill in with leaves and stems, masking first if necessary.*

6 *Stencil the sides of the table using the medium stencil alternately one way and then in reverse, overlapping a little and folding the edge to fit under the tabletop (p 22). Finally, varnish the whole table.*

Enlarge all the templates for this project to 167 per cent (see pages 18–19).

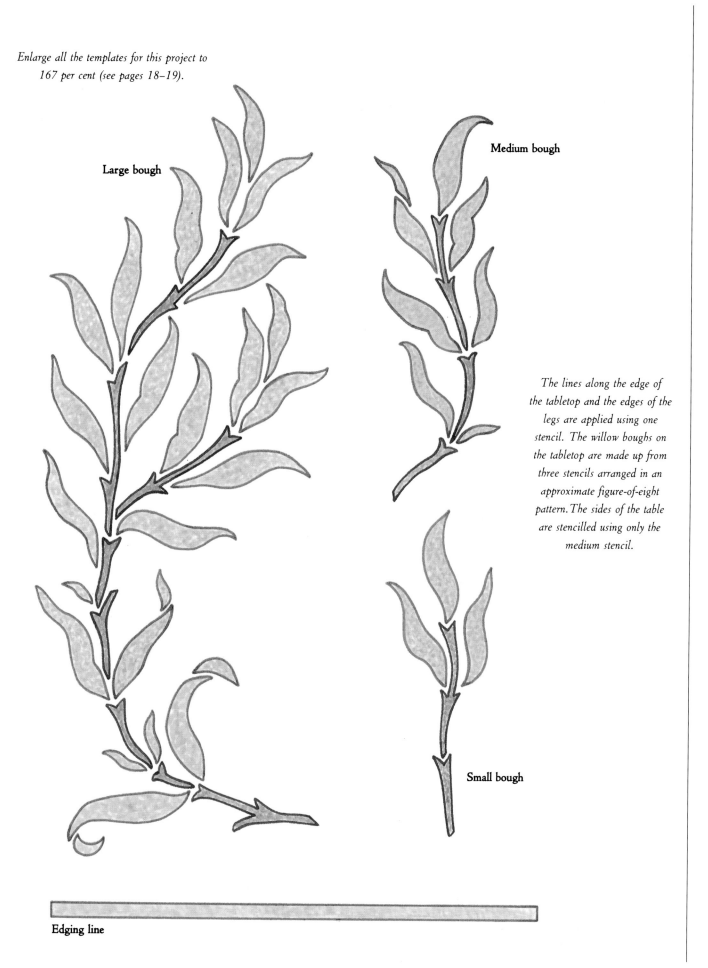

Large bough

Medium bough

The lines along the edge of the tabletop and the edges of the legs are applied using one stencil. The willow boughs on the tabletop are made up from three stencils arranged in an approximate figure-of-eight pattern. The sides of the table are stencilled using only the medium stencil.

Small bough

Edging line

Wild Rose Cushion Covers

This design fits an 18in- (46cm-) square cushion but could be enlarged or reduced for other sizes. It is stencilled onto the fabric square before being sewn. If you use acrylic paint, add a drop of fabric medium to make it more pliable. If you use fabric paints and fix them following the manufacturer's instructions, the cover will be hand-washable.

The design for these cushion (pillow) covers, depicting wild roses encircled by a leafy border, is taken from an embroidery design attributed to William Morris. With their rich colours and intricate pattern, the cushions will look good in a variety of styles of decor.

ABOVE AND OPPOSITE
The same stencils and paint colours were used for both of these cushions (though the pink petals on the green cushion are a deeper shade of pink than those on the red cushion). The contrasting background fabrics, however, create very different effects.

MATERIALS
Fabric such as glazed chintz
Fabric medium (if using acrylics)
Fabric or acrylic paints:
Pale green: cobalt, dark green, raw umber, white, ochre
Dark blue-green: cobalt, dark green, raw umber
Light pink: crimson, white
Deep pink: crimson, a little white
Mid green: ochre, dark green, white
Yellow: yellow, white

1 *Stretch the fabric taut, and tape all edges to your work surface, which you have protected with paper or plastic. Centre the flowers stencil on the fabric and tape in place. Stencil the inner border flowers in pale green. If you are using dark fabric you may have to apply a second coat, as the paint is absorbed into the fabric.*

T he design upon which this stencil is based is one of many that Morris's firm sold as ready-made cushions (pillows) and as embroidery kits, on both sides of the Atlantic. Morris had learned to embroider after studying medieval needlework, and he then trained his wife, daughter and friends. His stylized designs, worked in wool dyed with natural pigments and involving many long-forgotten stitches, were a notable departure from the unimaginative styles and gaudy colours popular at the time.

The wild-rose design has been changed very little in being adapted for stencilling. Two stencils are used, one involving four colours and the other three colours, with the dark blue-green shade used in both stencils. The stencils are arranged so as to separate interlocking portions of the design. This is easy to see in step 1, because the pencil lines visible on that stencil were used in designing the other.

2 *With the flowers stencil still in place on the fabric, mask off the lower edges of the flowers where they join the stems, so as not to risk smudging the flowers with paint. Stencil the stems and leaf veins using the dark blue-green paint, taking care to stencil right into the corners for a fine, sharp image.*

Flowers

Enlarge both templates for this project to
200 per cent (see pages 18–19).

Two interlocking stencils are used for this
design. The flowers stencil comprises the rose
flowers and stems, plus a little of the
surrounding border. The foliage stencil
includes the rest of the border, all the rose
leaves and the centres of
the roses.

3 Stencil the flowers in light pink using a
circular action and leaving the centre free
of paint. When dry, use a very small brush to
stencil around the outermost edges of the
flowers in deep pink.

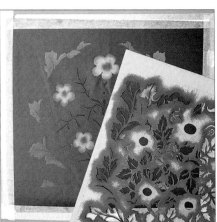

4 Carefully remove the flowers stencil and
replace it with the foliage stencil,
positioning it so that the flower centres fall
exactly in the centre of the petals and the
leaves line up. Tape in place.

Foliage

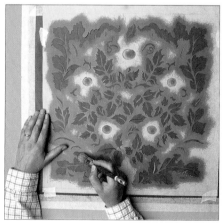

5 *Use dark blue-green to stencil the remainder of the border encircling the roses. Next to the pale green highlighted portions of the foliage stencilled in step 1, this dark green will look like a shadow.*

6 *Now stencil the rose leaves in mid green. If you have positioned the stencil correctly, the mid green parts of the leaves will fit exactly around the stems that you created in step 2.*

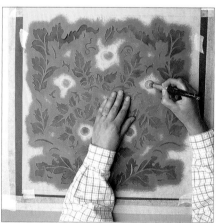

7 *Finally, stencil the yellow flower centres, which should fit exactly onto the flower centres that were left free of paint in step 3. Don't worry if there is some overlap with the light-pink paint.*

Daisy Design Wall Hanging

This stencilled canvas wall hanging would look striking in a living room, yet it could work equally well over a bedhead in the bedroom – indeed, the wall hanging that it is based on was embroidered by William Morris's wife for their own bedroom.

ABOVE AND OPPOSITE

Two stylized daisy motifs are used in an alternating pattern for this wall hanging. Pinks, yellows and cream are used for the flowers, and greens and blue for the stems and leaves. All the colours appear in the unusual geometric border.

This design was inspired by an indigo serge hanging embroidered in brightly coloured wool by Morris's wife, Janey, for their bedroom at the Red House in 1860, during the first year of their marriage. She worked the hanging from Morris's design.

Morris used the daisy motif in different forms on fabric, wallpaper and glass. His colleagues William de Morgan and Walter Crane also picked up on the daisy for use on tiles, on pottery and, in Crane's case, in illustrations and on wallpaper (see the Lily & Daisy Screen project on page 54). The Arts and Crafts movement was heavily influenced by medieval designs, and the daisy motif can be seen in early tapestries and medieval manuscripts.

This daisy motif could also be used singly on a small item such as a cushion surrounded by either the geometric border or just a single line. The border used here is taken from the border on an embroidered wool portiere by John Henry Dearle, the chief textile designer of Morris & Co, and it too was based on early tapestries.

The hanging is made from two layers of thin canvas dyed in the washing machine using beige and brown dye mixed together. The fabric pieces are stitched together and hanging loops inserted into the top edge. This one measures 67 x 39½in (170 x 100cm) but you could alter the dimensions by making the flowers a different size, using fewer, spacing them further apart or using more at the edge.

Before stencilling, use tailor's chalk to mark the border, which is about 3in (8cm) deep, and to mark the flowers, starting at the centre and working outwards.

Two types of daisy motif are used. One has soft yellow flowers, with strong-yellow stamens and green stems. The other has cream flowers with strong-yellow stamens, pink flowers and green stems with sharp pale-green tips. Both types have blue leaves.

Before you begin stencilling, it's a sensible precaution to protect your work surface with paper or plastic. Because fabric absorbs more paint, dilute each colour with a drop or two of fabric medium, in order to make the paint a workable consistency.

MATERIALS
Thin canvas dyed brown
Fabric medium
Acrylic or fabric paints:
Blue-green: Hooker's green, raw sienna, cerulean, white
Blue: ultramarine, cerulean, Payne's grey, raw umber
Sharp pale green: Hooker's green, raw sienna, cerulean, white, lemon yellow
Strong yellow: white, raw sienna, raw umber, Turner's yellow
Soft yellow: white, raw sienna, raw umber, Naples yellow
Pink: white, raw sienna, raw umber, permanent rose
Cream: white, raw sienna, raw umber

1 *Stencil a blue band all around the edges (p 23, step 1). Place the pentagon border stencil so that the bottoms of the windows are on the inner edge of the band. Stencil each pentagon in a different colour. Reposition the stencil so that the windows are between those already done, and stencil with different colours.*

2 *Place the triangle border stencil so that the triangles butt up to the stencilled shapes. Stencil the inner line in green and the triangles in blue. Reposition, and stencil blue triangles in between.*

3 *Stencil the flowers, alternating stencils. For both designs, the leaves are blue, the stems green (with sharp pale-green tips on one design) and the centres strong yellow. The flowers are soft yellow, pink or cream.*

4 *Before removing one stencil, position the other by butting it up to the first one. At the end of each row, mask off the areas not required. Position the rows so that the flowers are staggered.*

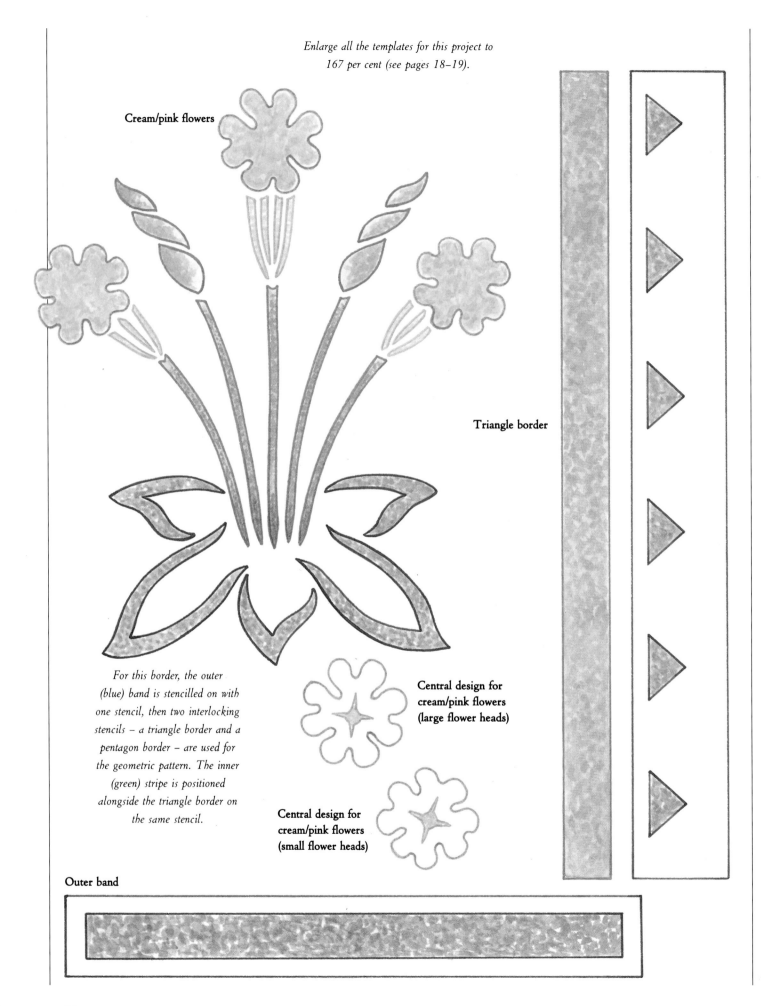

*Enlarge all the templates for this project to
167 per cent (see pages 18–19).*

Cream/pink flowers

Triangle border

*For this border, the outer
(blue) band is stencilled on with
one stencil, then two interlocking
stencils – a triangle border and a
pentagon border – are used for
the geometric pattern. The inner
(green) stripe is positioned
alongside the triangle border on
the same stencil.*

Central design for
cream/pink flowers
(large flower heads)

Central design for
cream/pink flowers
(small flower heads)

Outer band

Yellow flowers

Pentagon border

There is a stencil for the yellow daisies and another for the cream/pink ones. A large cut-out centre is used for the centres of the large yellow flowers, and a small one for those on the small yellow flowers. There is also a large and a small centre for the cream/pink flowers.

Central design for yellow flowers (large flower heads)

Central design for yellow flowers (small flower heads)

Lily & Daisy Screen

A wallpaper set by the illustrator Walter Crane was the inspiration for this large stencil design. Although the design is complex and some subtle shading is involved, it is not particularly difficult and the finished screen looks very impressive.

ABOVE AND OPPOSITE
In each panel of the screen, the daisies, interspersed with simple tufts of grass, are part of a decorative base filling the lower third of the panel. Above this sits a stylized vase of white lilies with soft pink edges.

This design is based upon two Walter Crane wallpapers, *The Lily and the Dove* and *La Margarete* (see page 11), which were designed to be used together. A third paper, not used here, represented the classical Greek myth of Alcestis.

Together, the papers made up an allegorical set, with the lilies symbolizing purity and the marguerite daisies innocence. Crane's daisy, which is very similar to William Morris's (see page 50), is medieval in style, and lines from the medieval poet Chaucer were woven into the design too.

In this stencil design, the lily has been simplified, but the grass pattern that appears in the background of Crane's paper is also used in the stencil. The sunflower border that separates the two areas is much the same as that used by Crane, though the stencilled version is larger. (You may need to make yours a different size to fit exactly into the panels of your screen.)

Be sure to plan the spacing of the motifs before painting the background colours, in case you need to raise or lower the dividing line. The daisy and grass stencils can also be used to cover the back of the screen.

The vase template is one half of the vase, as the stencil is turned over for the other half. Cut the stencil wider than this, as shown in step 7, to prevent a central "tidemark". Mark the centre on the stencil to aid in positioning.

MATERIALS

Emulsion (latex) paint in cinnamon and deep soft blue
Flat emulsion (latex) glaze
Flat acrylic varnish
Acrylic paints:
Greenish-brown: raw umber, raw sienna, a little white, a little Hooker's green
Blue-green: Prussian blue, raw sienna, a little Payne's grey, a little white
Olive green: Hooker's green, raw sienna, a little white
White: white, a little raw sienna, a little raw umber
Pink: crimson, raw umber, white
Orange: orange
Red: naphthol red, raw umber

1 *Stick 1in- (2.5cm-) wide tape across each panel, two-thirds of the way down. Paint blue emulsion (latex) above and cinnamon emulsion below it. When dry, remove the tape. Run more tape along each side of the white space; paint between in greenish-brown.*

2 *When dry, seal each panel with emulsion (latex) glaze. Paint the outer framework with the blue-green acrylic. Now stencil one panel at a time. For the daisy motifs, stencil the leaves and stems in olive green, applying it only lightly around the tips of the leaves.*

3 *Stencil each of the daisy flowers first in white. When this is dry, apply pink around the edges of these flowers. Finally, use the small cut-out circle stencil to paint the flower centres in orange.*

4 *Draw a line about ³⁄₈in (1cm) above the top of the windows in the sunflower border stencil. Position the stencil by lining this up with the bottom edge of the greenish-brown line dividing the upper and lower portions of the panel. Fold the end of the stencil to protect the outer framework of the screen from smudges.*

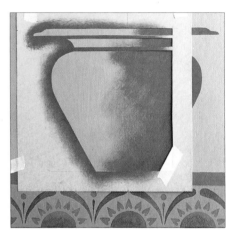

5 *Stencil the sunflower border using the olive green for the heart-shaped flower petals and the small circles. Mix the olive green with blue-green for the flower centres and use the blue-green on its own elsewhere.*

6 *Add a row of olive-green grass above the higher daisy motif, another row beneath the lower daisies and a third row between the first two. Dot individual grass motifs evenly between these rows.*

7 *Position the vase stencil. Brush in red then turn the stencil over to do the other side before the first has dried. Keep the centre light, and darken the edges by adding more raw umber to the red paint.*

8 *Using the lower stem stencil, paint three olive-green stems with blue-green leaves, starting with the central one and turning the stencil over for the third. Slant the outer stems outwards slightly.*

9 *The upper stem stencil is used to extend the top of each stem. Paint the left side of the central stem first, using the same colours as in step 8. You will need to plan the position of the stencil carefully.*

10 *Again using the blue-green and olive-green, turn the upper stem stencil over and paint the right side of the central stem. Stencil the righthand stem, then turn it over and do the lefthand stem.*

11 *Use the double-bud stencil and then the single-bud stencil to apply the central flower buds, stencilling the leaves and stems as before, and the flower buds white with soft pink edges.*

12 *Brush in the flowers on the other three stems using the flower stencil. Do the leaf and stem only where needed. Add orange stamens. Fill in awkward spaces with single leaves.*

13 *Use the single-bud stencil to add the remaining buds. Turn the stencil over and repeat steps 12–13 for the other side. Repeat the whole procedure for the other two panels, then varnish the screen.*

Daisy motif

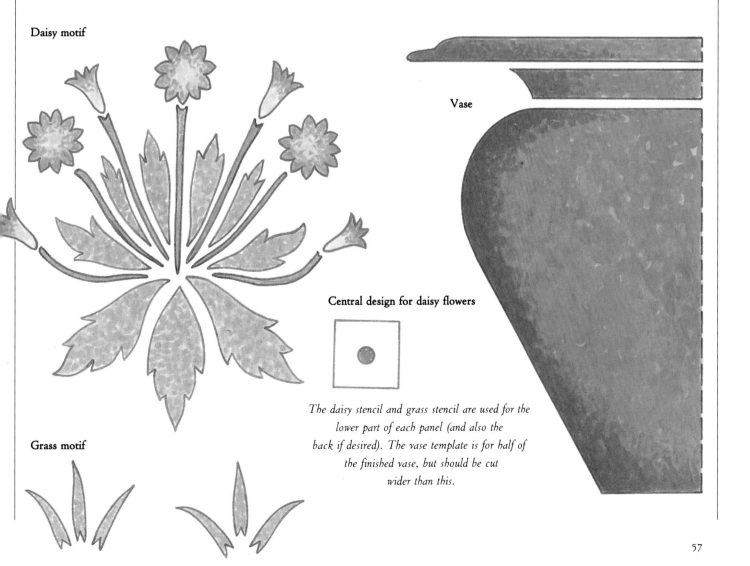

Vase

Central design for daisy flowers

Grass motif

The daisy stencil and grass stencil are used for the lower part of each panel (and also the back if desired). The vase template is for half of the finished vase, but should be cut wider than this.

*Enlarge all the templates for this project to
167 per cent (see pages 18–19).*

*The two lily stem stencils are joined to form a
long stem; both sides of the stencils are used.
The sunflower border is repeated across
the panels.*

Lower lily stem

Upper lily stem

Sunflower border

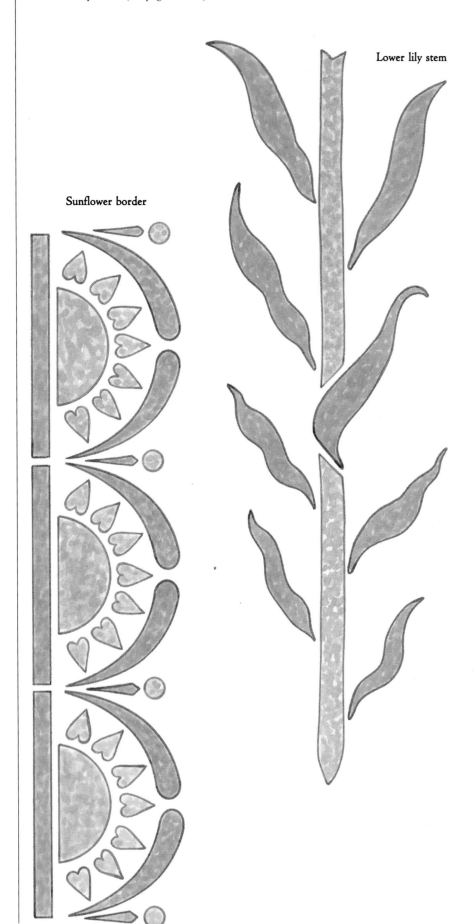

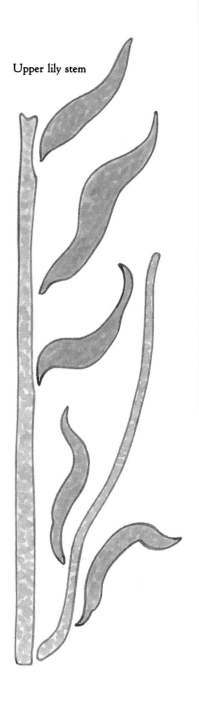

*The lily flower and bud stencils fit
onto the tips of the stems. Use one side
of the flower stencil for one side of the design,
then turn it over for the
other side.*

Double lily bud

Single lily bud

Lily flower

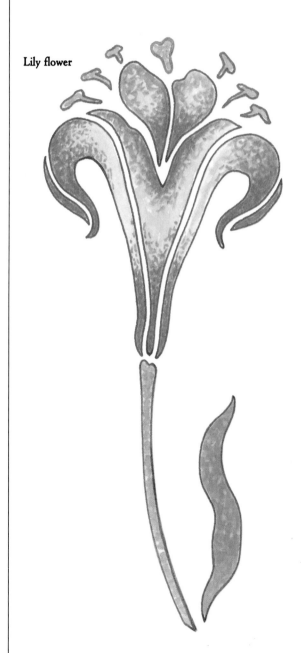

DINING ROOMS & KITCHENS

The dining room is a good place to try out a bold stencilled effect. The two dining room projects in this chapter are both very dramatic in their own way. The colourful, highly decorated dresser (hutch) overleaf is one of the most intricate projects in the book, while the black and gold circular table (page 68) is probably the most elegant. Other surfaces that could be stencilled in a dining room include curtains, a sideboard (buffet), floorboards and, of course, the walls. In a kitchen, stencilling can be used to define areas. The tile-effect stencil (page 76) makes an attractive alternative to tiles, while the stencilled café curtain (page 72) looks lovely and fresh in either a kitchen or a bathroom. Other opportunities for stencilling in the kitchen include wooden cupboards, painted or natural pine shelves, plate racks and dressers, the floor and a variety of wooden accessories, from spice racks to kitchen roll holders.

Fruit Design Dresser & Mats

The panels on this dresser (hutch) and the matching placemats have a hand-painted look. Inspired by panels in a room decorated by William Morris's firm, the highly decorated doors of the dresser contrast dramatically with the simple shelves above.

ABOVE AND OPPOSITE
Each panel on the dresser (hutch) and on the four placemats depicts a different fruit. The "painterly" quality is achieved through careful shading and highlighting, hand-painted detailing and the lack of ties, which are filled in by hand.

In 1866 the South Kensington Museum in London (now the Victoria & Albert Museum) commissioned William Morris's fledgling company to decorate a room there. The Green Dining Room was an important commission for the firm and can still be seen today at the museum, where it is called the William Morris Room. As part of the decoration of the room, Edward Burne-Jones and Charles Fairfax-Murray painted panels along the top of the wainscoting. Depicting fruit against a gold background, the panels were the inspiration for the stencilled fruit panels on this dresser and the matching placemats. The motifs surrounding the panels on the dresser were inspired by a heavily patterned cabinet designed in 1858 by William Burges and now also in the William Morris Room.

The step-by-step instructions here are for the dresser (hutch). The placemats are done in the same way as the

dresser door panels, though with a different border. Cork is lovely to stencil on, but it is very absorbent, so take care not to smudge the paint – mistakes are difficult to remove. Seal the placemats with two coats of flat polyurethane varnish to protect them from heat and moisture.

The dresser is painted with emulsion (latex) paint prior to stencilling. After stencilling, it is coated with acrylic varnish, which has been tinted with raw umber to tone down the colours. Furniture polish may be applied if desired.

MATERIALS
Eggshell paint in brownish-red and yellow shades
Flat acrylic varnish tinted with raw umber (for dresser)
Flat polyurethane varnish (for placemats)
Acrylic paints:
Dark green: Hooker's green, Payne's grey, raw umber
Light pink: white, a very small amount of crimson
Medium pink: white, crimson
Yellow-green: Hooker's green, Turner's yellow
Mustard: burnt umber
Red: crimson, raw umber, a little white
Purple: crimson, raw umber, Payne's grey, violet
Yellow: Naples yellow
Light green: Hooker's green, Naples yellow

1 *First paint the dresser (hutch). Use brownish-red eggshell for everything except the door panels. Paint the panels in yellow eggshell. Paint the inner edges of the mouldings around the panels by hand, using the dark-green paint and a fine artist's brush.*

2 *Fold the edges of the pear stencil so that it fits exactly into one panel; tape in place if necessary. Mask off the flowers and fruit if you wish, using a piece of card. Paint the leaves and stems using the dark green. Do not even out the paint.*

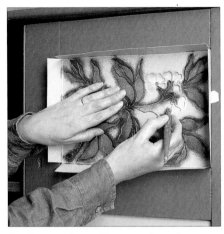

3 *Remove the masking tape from the flowers and the pears, if you have used it. Softly stencil the centre of each petal with light pink and the edges with a medium pink, to make the flowers stand out.*

4 *Stencil the fruit in yellow-green, stippling the edges with a slightly deeper shade to add texture. Leave a small spot in the centre of each pear so that the yellow undercoat shows through as a highlight.*

5 *Remove the stencil and finish with hand-painting. Fill in the ties with smooth lines of dark green. Paint leaf veins with burnt umber. Add burnt umber dots for the flower stamens and pear markings.*

6 *On the other panels stencil yellow-green apples, red cherries and purple figs. Using burnt umber, hand-paint dots on the apples and ridges on the figs, and add a red split in some figs.*

7 *Hand-paint dark-green lines along the top and base. Stencil three flowers along the plinth, using the stencil in full at the centre and masking off its top and the two lower dots in the other positions.*

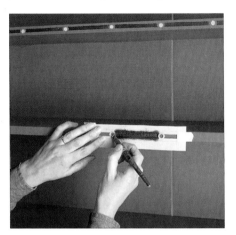

8 *For the shelf edges use the line-and-dot stencil. Start from the centre with a dot, and work out to the edges, going over the dots again to strengthen the colour if necessary. Varnish.*

Enlarge all the templates for this project to 167 per cent (see pages 18–19).

LEFT

The placemats are cork, and the stencilling is done in the same acrylic colours as used on the dresser. Each of the four placemats is different, with the central design the same as one of the four panels on the dresser, depicting cherries, apples, pears or figs. The border is used only on the placemats.

9 *Stencil the horizontal bands between the door panels in yellow using the horizontal stencil. Now use the cut-out flower shape to stencil the brownish-red dot of emulsion (latex) in the flower centre.*

10 *Use the vertical-band stencil on both sides of each panel, and only the top portion of the stencil at the bottom. Stencil it all in yellow, and then go over the leaves using light green paint.*

11 *Remove the vertical-band stencil and replace it with the outline stencil, taking care to position the windows exactly over the yellow portions. Stencil in dark green to outline all the yellow shapes.*

For the dresser, there are stencils for the four fruit panels and also stencils for the horizontal band (plus a centre dot), vertical band (plus an outline), plinth and shelf edges. For each placemat, use a fruit stencil and the border.

Central design for flower

Horizontal band

Vertical band

Placemat border

Plinth motifs

Outline for vertical band

Cherries panel

Pears panel

66

Line-and-dot shelf edging

Apples panel

Figs panel

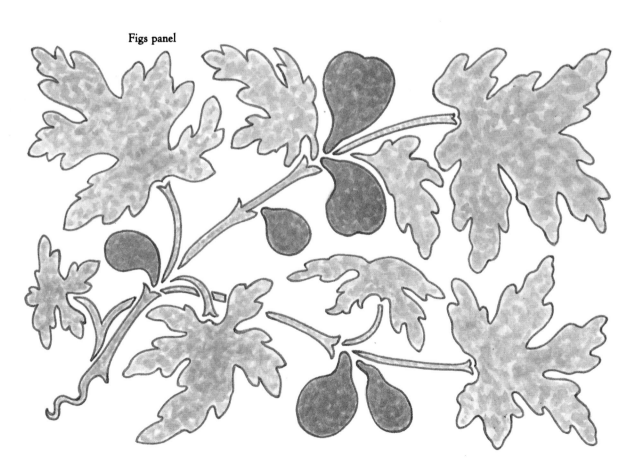

Oak & Acorn Dining Table

MATERIALS
Emulsion (latex) paint in flat black
Flat emulsion (latex) glaze
Acrylic medium
Flat acrylic varnish
Acrylic paints:
Ivory: white, raw sienna
Brownish-red: red oxide
Ochre: raw sienna mixed with acrylic medium
Gold: water-based reddish gold

Based on a woodcut designed by William Morris for the Kelmscott Chaucer, *this intricate circular stencil will turn a plain table into an elegant piece of furniture. The colours of ivory, red oxide and gold look stunning against the matt black background.*

ABOVE AND OPPOSITE
Intertwining oak leaves and acorns decorate both the central motif and the border of this design for a circular table. It could be enlarged or reduced and could be used on a tablecloth instead of a table. Hand-painted gold detailing adds richness.

This oak leaf design was inspired by one of the woodcut borders in the *Kelmscott Chaucer*, designed by Morris to surround woodcut illustrations by Burne-Jones. The book was published four months before Morris's death by the Kelmscott Press, which he had founded in 1891. This border is from the Tale of the Clerk of Oxenford.

Morris's border is rectangular but in other respects the stencil design is very similar. The use of the ivory paint against the black background of the table recreates the feeling of the white-on-black woodcut. The oak and acorn design is well suited to the border of a circular dining table, with a simplified version used in the middle. This table is 5 feet (1.5 metres) across, so if yours is larger or smaller, you will need to adjust the dimensions of the stencil.

Flat varnish is essential to protect the surface. Furniture polish can be applied if desired, to give a soft sheen.

1 *Paint the table with black emulsion (latex); sand with steel wool till smooth. Seal with emulsion (latex) glaze. Mark the centre with chalk, then place the hole in the middle of the central stencil over the mark. Stencil the leaves with two coats of ivory, and the lines and central dot in brownish-red.*

2 *Still using the central stencil, very softly brush the ochre paint, which you have thinned with acrylic medium, over parts of the leaves and acorns. The effect should be very subtle, so don't apply the paint too heavily or evenly. The aim of this step is to make the design look like old ivory.*

3 With the two cut-out leaf centres, stencil the leaf veins lightly in brownish-red. Use a very small brush for this, and take particular care to get right into the corners of the stencil so that none of the fine detailing at the tips of the leaf veins is lost.

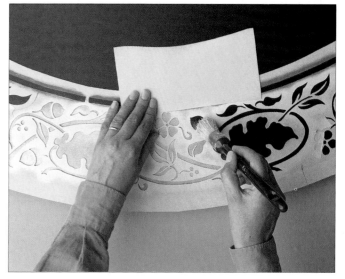

4 Use the outer stencil to paint each segment of the border around the rim of the table. Start with two coats of ivory, masking out the inner line with a piece of card. Make sure that the design fits in evenly all around; you may have to make a few slight adjustments so that it will fit exactly around the rim.

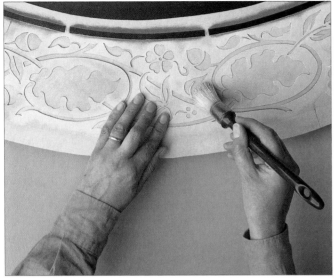

5 *Once again, lightly brush the ivory paint with a little ochre thinned with a drop or two of acrylic medium. Still using the outer stencil, paint the inner line in brownish-red, masking off any portions of the ivory that are very close. Use the cut-out leaf centres to stencil the leaf veins in brownish-red.*

6 *Finally, paint over the brownish-red lines by hand with gold paint. Smooth the gold on lightly so the brownish-red shows through. Dot small gold spots on the acorn cups. If desired, you can also hand-paint the outer rim in brownish-red with gold on top. Finish with two coats of flat acrylic varnish.*

Veins for leaves

Enlarge all the templates for this project to 250 per cent (see pages 18–19).

The cut-out centre from each oak leaf is used for stencilling the leaf veins. Use these veins on each cut-out centre.

Outer border

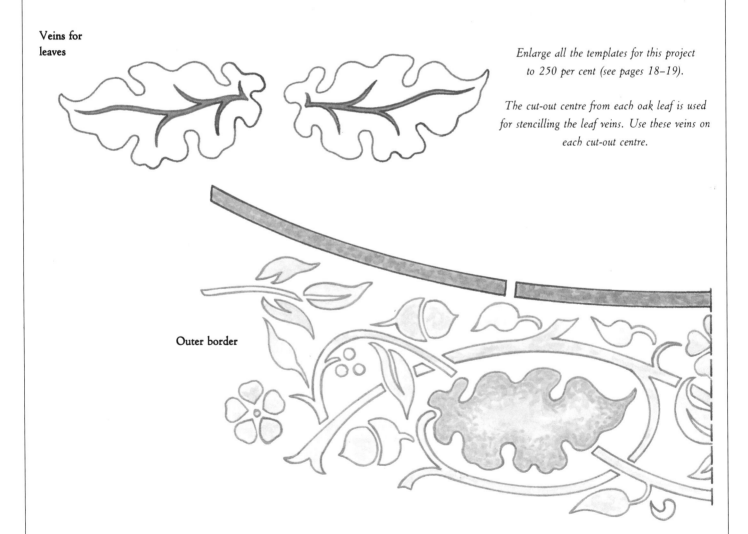

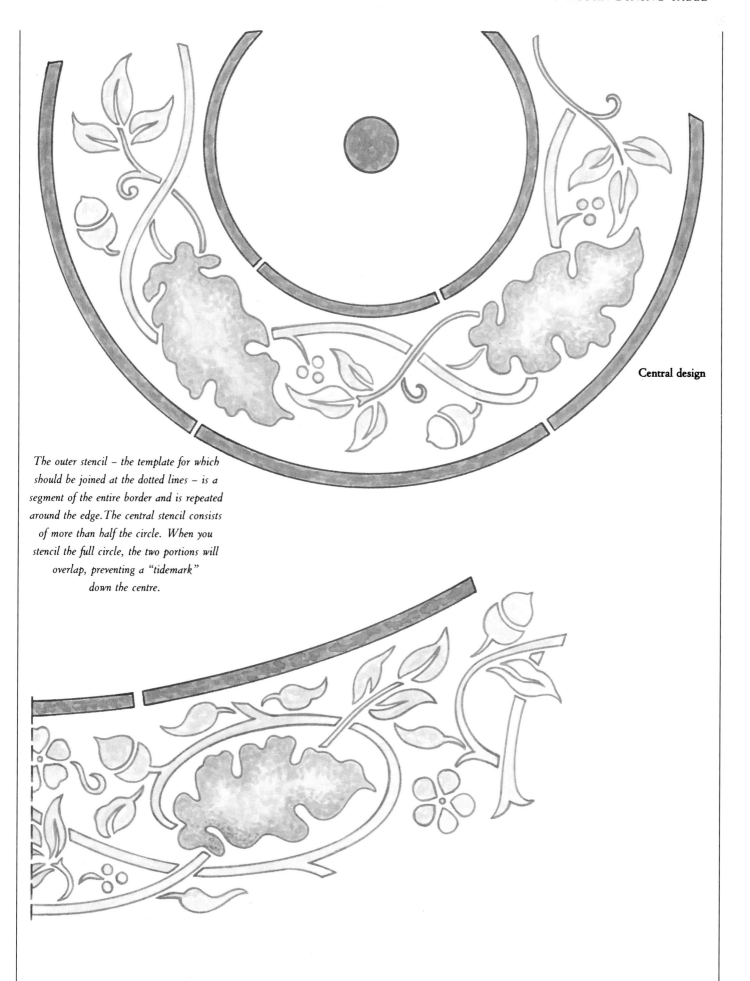

Central design

The outer stencil – the template for which should be joined at the dotted lines – is a segment of the entire border and is repeated around the edge. The central stencil consists of more than half the circle. When you stencil the full circle, the two portions will overlap, preventing a "tidemark" down the centre.

Cornflower Café Curtain

The light filtering through this cotton lawn café curtain adds to the rather ethereal effect of these stencilled cornflowers and grasses. Although inspired by a tile by William de Morgan, the diagonal design works equally well on fabric.

ABOVE AND OPPOSITE
In this design, lines of cornflowers and grasses run diagonally across the fabric in opposite directions. The lightly brushed-in grasses, and the bolder flowers on top, create a sense of movement. A wide band and a narrow one around the side and top edges frame the design.

The design for this soft, flowing curtain fabric is based on a 6in (15cm) red-lustre tile by William de Morgan. There is a freshness about the brushstrokes on the tile which turns it into a perfect textile design. The two layers – grasses and flowers – give movement to the design, making it look like a whole field of flowers.

As there is only one colour for each stencil in this design, it is a fairly simple project to do, although the end result is surprisingly complex-looking. Cool greens and blues are used here, but it would look good in other colour-ways too, such as soft brownish-red for the flowers and yellow for the grasses, and the design would also be suitable for a tablecloth or bedspread.

The fabric is stencilled before being made up into a curtain, so allow enough fabric for the side and lower hems and the heading. It is advisable to practise on an extra piece to

get used to the fine, loosely woven cloth. The curtains are hand-washable because the fabric paints are fixed by ironing (using a cloth and following the manufacturer's instructions) after being stencilled.

Before preparing the stencils, draw two vertical and two horizontal lines about 8½in (22cm) apart on the cornflower stencil card. On the grasses stencil card, draw three vertical and three horizontal lines about 4¼in (11cm) apart. Use the grids to help you space the repeat motifs equally and at the correct angle.

Protect your work surface with paper or a plastic sheet, as the paint will soak through thin fabric. Stick the cloth to the work surface with masking tape along all edges, making sure it is square and as taut as possible.

MATERIALS
Cotton lawn (or similar) curtain fabric in white or a pale colour
Tailor's chalk
Fabric paints:
Green: light green, white, a little burnt sienna
Blue: ultramarine, white, a little burnt sienna

1 *Using the border stencil, apply the two blue bands (p 23) around the side and lower edges, taking care not to pull the cloth. You will find that a stroking motion in only one direction works best.*

2 *Decide on the position of the first diagonal line of grasses across the bottom right corner of the fabric. Using either a set square (carpenter's square) or triangular piece of card, draw a diagonal line with tailor's chalk. This can later be brushed off.*

3 *Lay the grasses stencil across the corner, lining up the line you have pencilled on the stencil with the one you have drawn in tailor's chalk on the fabric. Use masking tape to mask out where the windows overlap the border, so that the grasses will stop just short of the inner band.*

4 *Lightly stencil the grasses in green, being careful not to move the cloth at all, then lift the stencil and reposition, using your eye to line it up with the grasses just completed. Continue stencilling the grasses in the same way over all the fabric, masking any new areas that overlap the border.*

5 *Position the other stencil at the bottom right so that the pencilled lines align with the lines drawn on the fabric. Mask any windows overlapping the border. Stencil in blue, then reposition using the flowers on the stencil edges as a registration guide. Stencil the whole cloth. When dry, fix the colours by ironing over a cloth.*

Enlarge all the templates for this project to 250 per cent (see pages 18–19).

One stencil is used for the two bands of the border, another for the grasses and a third for the cornflowers. Make the grasses and cornflowers stencils big enough to include two of each motif. The partial flowers on the edges of the cornflowers stencil are to use for registration when repositioning the stencil.

Grasses motif

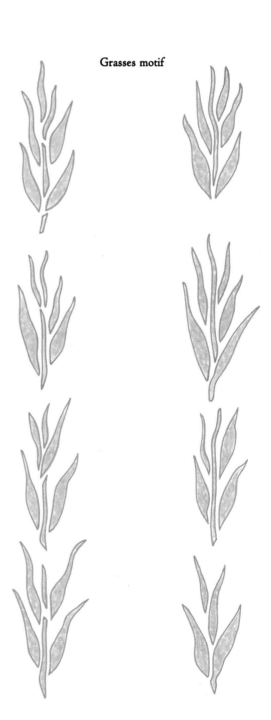

Border

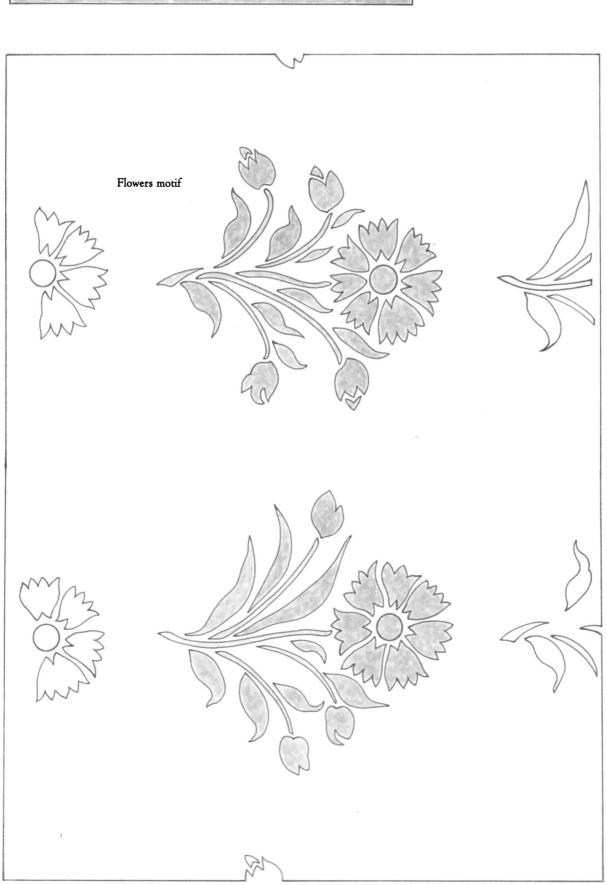

Flowers motif

Swan & Sprig Tile Pattern

This stencil pattern reproduces the effect of ceramic tiles and could be used in a pantry or kitchen, or around a bath. The design is based on hand-painted tiles by the influential Arts and Crafts architect and designer Philip Webb.

ABOVE AND OPPOSITE

This blue tile-pattern stencil is made up of a swan motif and a leafy sprig, arranged chequerboard-fashion and surrounded by a scroll-pattern border. Hand-painted pink "grouting" and a yellow line inside the border add to the illusion.

The blue-and-white tiles from which this stencil design is taken appear on a chimney-hood over a fireplace in the Old Hall at Queen's College, Cambridge. Designed by Philip Webb, a founding partner in William Morris's company, they were produced for the college by the firm in 1862. The tiles form a background to highly decorated tile panels depicting The Months.

Morris particularly liked blue-and-white tiles and they were often used in this way during the company's early years. In fact, in another 1862 overmantel produced by the firm, the same Philip Webb tiles were used with six elaborate tiles by the painter and designer Edward Burne-Jones illustrating the story of Beauty and the Beast.

Each of the Webb tiles is divided up into 16 tiny squares containing either swans or leafy sprigs. For this stencil design, the swans and sprigs have been enlarged to the size

of individual tiles. The hand-painted pink lines between them resemble grouting. The original fireplace panel is surrounded by blue-and-white border tiles, bearing a pattern similar to the motif on the border in this project. A yellowish line runs along the inner edge of the border tiles on the fireplace panel, and a corresponding hand-painted yellow line is used in this project inside the border.

The stencil will look good in a farmhouse-style or cottage-style kitchen or bathroom, yet it will also work surprisingly well with a modern decor in soft colours. If you wish to re-create the blue-and-white colour scheme, you can stencil in blue onto a white emulsioned (latexed) surface. However, pale-blue emulsion is also effective and looks a little softer, as can be seen in the photograph opposite. Similarly, a pale blue colourwashed wall (see page 17) would make an attractive background. And because the surface is varnished after stencilling, it makes an alternative to tiles that is practical as well as attractive.

One other advantage of this stencil is its versatility, as it can be used in a small area such as behind a stove or on a box lid, or it can cover a whole wall. Enlarging or reducing the template a little on a photocopier will help you to ensure the design fits into the given space exactly.

MATERIALS

Emulsion (latex) paint in light blue or white
Flat polyurethane varnish
Acrylic paints:
Blue: ultramarine, white, Payne's grey, a very small amount of crimson
Yellow: Turner's yellow, Naples yellow
Pink: white, red oxide

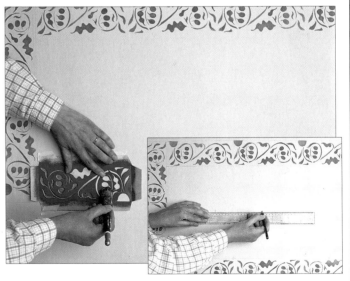

1 *Use a pencil, ruler, spirit level and set square (carpenter's square) to mark the outer lines of the area you will be stencilling, making sure that complete swan and sprig motifs will fit inside the border without too much space in between. Stencil the border in blue.*
INSET: Draw lines just inside it, then draw lines for the horizontal edges of the swan/sprig tiles. Measure and mark the vertical edges.

2 Use a set square to draw in the vertical lines you have marked so that each segment of this pencilled grid will actually be square. It doesn't matter that the pencil lines will show after you have finished – they will make the pink "grouting" look more realistic, thereby adding to the tile effect.

3 Position the sprig stencil so that it is centred in the top left square of your grid, and secure it in place with masking tape. (All the sprigs will be stencilled with the motifs facing in the same direction.) Using a fairly large brush and a circular motion, stencil the sprig in blue, keeping the paint soft and light.

4 Remove the sprig stencil and tape the swan stencil next to it. Stencil the swan in blue, applying the paint very thinly in the centre. Continue stencilling the sprig and swan alternately, varying the density of paint.

5 Place the line stencil centrally over the line you've pencilled just inside the border. Stencil in yellow with a circular action, softening the colour before the end of the stencil. Before the paint has dried, reposition the stencil so that it overlaps the softened portion a little, and continue stencilling along all four edges.

6 Using the pencilled lines between the squares as guide lines, paint in pink "grouting" by hand. A slightly wobbly line will add to the tile-like appearance. In addition, paint pink lines between the border repeats so that the border looks like rectangular tiles; the pink lines should go over the top of the painted yellow lines.

7 As well as hand-painting pink lines between the tiles, you need to add grouting inside the yellow line all the way around, and also along the very outer edge of the border tiles. You can paint in the grouting in this step and the previous step in whatever sequence you find most convenient. Finally, varnish with polyurethane.

*Enlarge all the templates for this project to
167 per cent (see pages 18–19).*

*There is a stencil for each of the "tiles" in this
design: a swan motif and a sprig, both
of which are square tiles, and a rectangular
border tile. There is also a stencil for
the line inside the border.*

**Scroll-pattern
border**

Sprig

Inner line

Swan

BEDROOMS & BATHROOMS

The bed, being the biggest piece of furniture in the bedroom, makes a good starting point for a decorating scheme. The project on page 82 provides a stencil you can use on both a bedstead and a bed cover. The delicate floral stencil on page 93 can be used to decorate anything from a lampshade to all four walls of the bedroom. Or, instead of stencilling entire walls, the animal frieze project (page 88) is quick and looks charming in a child's bedroom; it can also be used on furniture such as a toy chest. In the bathroom, the bath panelling is often crying out for decoration, and the stencil on page 104 provides a design that would make any bathroom seem a haven of luxury. If you have an unpatterned floor, the ornate floorcloth (page 98) would make a striking focal point; alternatively, you could just stencil the bathroom cabinet.

Floral Medallion Bed Design

This bed cover is based on William Morris's own, which was designed and embroidered by his wife, probably for his sixtieth birthday. The bed itself is decorated in much the same colours, using the flower motif from the bed cover.

ABOVE AND OPPOSITE
Floral medallions are stencilled all over this bed cover in yellow, maroon and blue-green fabric dyes. A maroon and yellow border runs around the edges. The same flowers are stencilled in maroon and green acrylic paints onto the blue-green painted bedstead.

Morris's magnificent four-poster bed at Kelmscott Manor, his home in Oxfordshire, was hung with curtains and a valance designed and embroidered by his daughter May. The bed cover was by his wife, Janey, and featured a variety of flowers, including the daisy, a repeat of Janey's first embroidered hanging (see page 50).

Only one flower is used on this stencilled bed cover, but the medallion design is very similar. This border is also much the same as the original, though it has been enlarged.

The bed cover is easy to sew. You will need to join widths to make it wide enough, so make sure that the seam runs exactly down the centre. Stitch a double hem all around.

This bed cover measures 96 x 98in (244 x 249cm) but you could enlarge or reduce the stencil, or space the medallions further apart, so the design would fit a different size of cover exactly. Plan the spacing of the medallions before

you cut out the stencils, because you need to allow for the space between them on the medallion stencil. As this stencil is quite delicate, varnish it on both sides for strength. Protect your work surface with plastic sheeting or newspaper. When stencilling the border, stretch the fabric taut and then tape the edges to your work surface. Working on one area at a time is easier than attempting to secure large areas at once. Taping the edges will not be necessary when stencilling the main part of the design.

MATERIALS
Heavy cotton bed cover in a light colour
Varnish (for sealing medallion stencil)
Fabric dyes:
Maroon: crimson, burnt sienna
Yellow: yellow, white
Blue-green: Blue, green, a little white

1 *Stretch the fabric taut and tape the lower left corner to your work surface. Position the outer border stencil at the corner as shown, aligning with the edge of the fabric. Mark where the lower edge of the inner line in the adjacent border will come to, and mask out the end of the inner line from this point.*

2 *Stencil all unmasked windows in maroon. Move the stencil along a little and fill in the ties while the paint is still wet. Remove the tape and position the stencil horizontally as shown. Mask out the first short diagonal line as well as the end of the inner line. Stencil in maroon, again filling in the ties.*

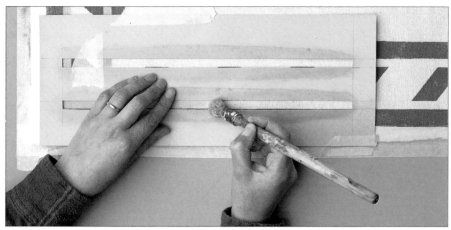

3 *Continue to the end of the taped area, then go back to the original corner and place the inner border stencil inside the maroon border, masking the inner lines at the corner as before. Stencil in yellow, softening the ends (p 23, step 1). Continue in the same way. At the end, adjust the spacing a little if necessary.*

4 *Using tailor's chalk, mark the centre point of the bed cover. Position the central diamond of the medallion stencil over this, and stencil in yellow. (Do not stencil the diamond, which is a registration mark.)*

5 *To help you reposition the stencil for each repeat, mark some more registration marks on each edge of the stencil to indicate where the adjacent motifs begin. Line one set of marks up with a previously stencilled medallion, and stencil in yellow. Stencil yellow medallions over the entire bed cover.*

6 *Position the flower stencil inside the central medallion. Using a ruler, mark the centre line (which should be in line with the seamline of the bed cover) by drawing a line or cutting notches at each end. Also mark registration lines on each edge of the stencil to indicate the position of the medallion.*

LEFT
Each panel of the bed is stencilled using only the flower stencil. For the centre panel, shown here, the stencil is used twice, with the flowers facing in opposite directions. For each side panel the stencil is used just once, but facing the opposite way from the one on the other side panel.

7 Use the central line or notches and the registration marks to position the flower stencil within each medallion. Paint in the stems and leaves in blue-green. The tips of the leaves and stems are very narrow, so make sure that you get the paint right into the corners for a fine, crisp effect.

8 Stencil the flowers in maroon before moving on to the next medallion. Don't worry if the paint smudges onto the leaves a little, as this softens the flowers attractively. Stencil the other medallions in the same way, using both sides of the stencil. Fix the dyes following the manufacturer's instructions.

Enlarge all the templates for this project to 250 per cent (see pages 18–19).

Cut the flower stencil wide enough to allow you to make registration marks on it. Both sides of the stencil are used, so for speed and convenience you may wish to cut two – one for each side.

Flower motif

The medallion stencil needs to be cut with a wide-enough margin for you to mark registration lines for the beginning of the next stencil (see step 5). The central diamond, which is for registration, should be cut out but not stencilled.

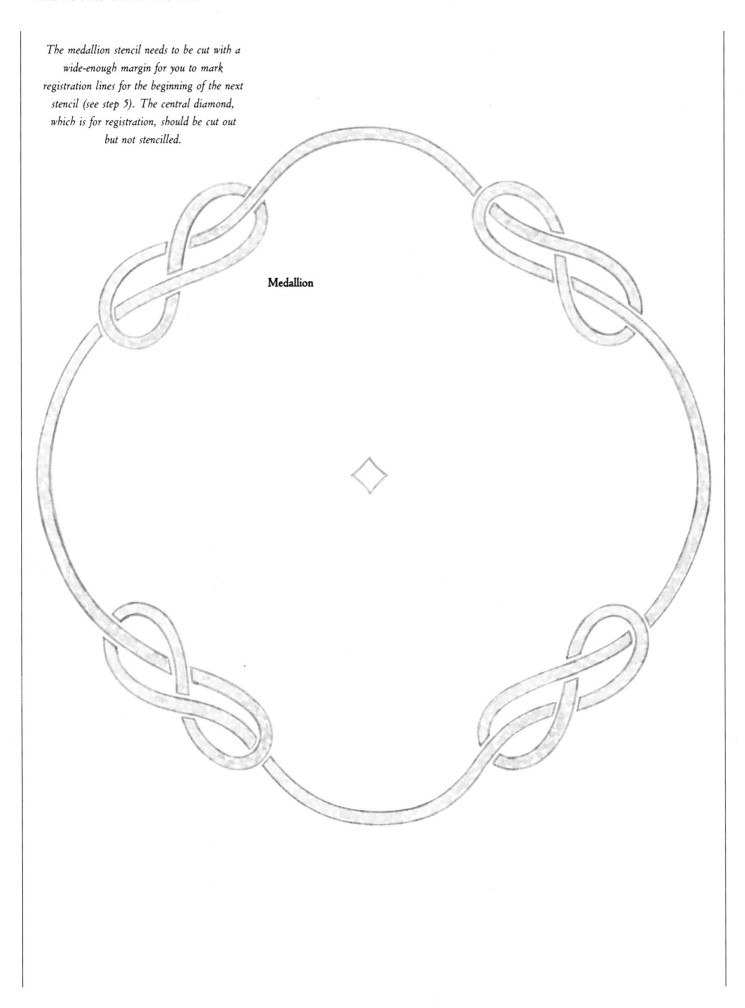

Medallion

The outer border stencil is used all around the edge of the bed cover. The inner border stencil, with the two narrow stripes, fits inside it.

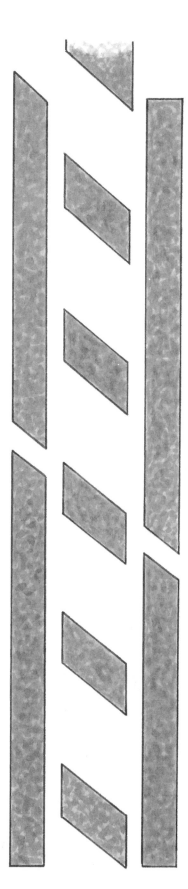

Outer border stencil

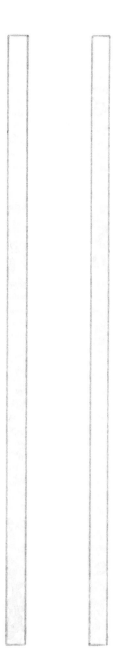

Inner border stencil

Animal Frieze & Toy Chest

*Based on a tapestry border by the designer Heywood
Sumner, this playful design of animals bounding
through foliage is perfect for a frieze running around
a child's room but can also be easily adapted
to fit onto a toy chest.*

ABOVE AND RIGHT
*The flower motif alternates with the animal panel in the frieze.
On the toy chest the flowers are omitted and the animals and border are
arranged to fit the area. The colour combinations, too, are
similar but not identical.*

The border that inspired this stencil is part of *The Chase*
tapestry by the Arts and Crafts designer Heywood
Sumner. The tapestry was woven in 1908 by Morris & Co
at their Merton Abbey works in Surrey.

The design of the frieze is based on a border of alternating rectangles and squares. Each rectangle surrounds the
scene of animals and foliage, which is sinuous and inter-
twined and has a feeling of movement. The squares
interspersed between these panels contain stylized flowers.
The contrast between the flowing animal panels and the
static flowers gives the frieze a pleasing visual rhythm.

The toy chest incorporates elements of the frieze on the
sides and lid. Both the border and the animal panel have
been adapted to fit the chest and the design is therefore
much freer than the frieze. Here is a chance to play about
with the stencil and use all or part of it.

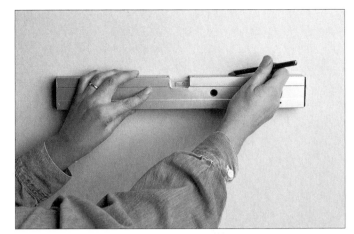

MATERIALS

Medium to large natural sponge
Flat emulsion (latex) glaze
Acrylic medium
Flat acrylic varnish
Acrylic paints:
Pale blue: white, a little cerulean blue,
a little raw umber
Green: Hooker's green mixed with a little
acrylic medium
Turquoise: cerulean blue, raw umber, a little white mixed with a
little acrylic medium

1 *Using a spirit level (carpenter's level) and a pencil, lightly mark the top and bottom edges of the frieze, then apply masking tape outside those lines. Measure your animal stencil and mark where the squares that go between the animal panels will be.*

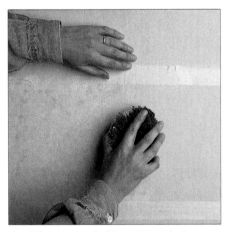

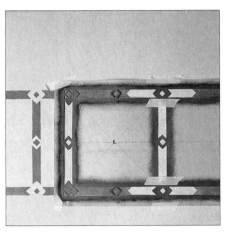

2 *Thin some pale blue paint with glaze and put on a large plate. Press the sponge lightly onto it then dab it on the wall between the lengths of tape.*

3 *Position the border stencil on the first square and stencil it in green, also stencilling a little beyond it. Move the stencil to the right and repeat for the next square.*

4 *Use the horizontal bands in the stencil to fill in between the squares with green, centring the diamonds. Use the V-shaped ends for the left side of the righthand square.*

Enlarge all the templates for this project to 250 per cent (see pages 18–19).

When tracing the template for the animal stencil, join the two sections at the dotted lines to form one stencil. For the toy chest, use the whole stencil plus half the stencil again to make a wider panel.

Animal panel

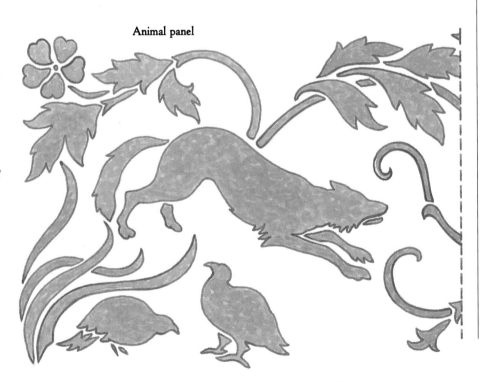

5 *Continue around the room. Now, using the square flower stencil, stencil a turquoise flower inside one green square. Do not remove the stencil yet.*

6 *When the turquoise is dry, place the cut-out centre from the flower stencil on top, and apply pale blue. Stencil the other squares in the same way.*

7 *Place the animal stencil between the squares. Apply turquoise, keeping the paint light in the middle of the animals. Repeat around the room.*

**Individual animal
stencils for
toy chest**

8 *Remove the animal stencil and paint in the animals' eyes in pale blue, using a very fine paintbrush. If you wish to protect your handiwork from children's fingerprints, apply a coat of flat acrylic varnish over the whole frieze.*

If desired, cut out individual animal stencils to provide greater flexibility in making the animal panel fit the toy chest.

The square part of the border fits
around the flower motif exactly, while horizontal
lines are stencilled to fit above and below the animal
panels. The V-shaped ends of
the lines form part of the diamonds at the
corners of the subsequent square.

Border

Flower motif

**Central design for
flower motif**

Floral Wall & Lampshade

Based on a wallpaper by William Morris, this flower pattern is equally suited to the walls of a bedroom or to the shade on a simple bedside lamp.
The stencilled border can be used to frame walls, windows or doorways.

ABOVE
In this design a border, stencilled on a painted blue band, runs around the edges of the walls. As well as a sprig motif, there are four flowers – a mauve/yellow pansy and a pink/yellow daisy (both seen here), a mauve/yellow aster and a pink/white carnation.

The flowers in this design were inspired by *Powdered*, an 1874 William Morris wallpaper design used in a bedroom at Standen, a house in Sussex designed by Philip Webb and decorated by Morris. The original had a willow background, which is represented here by the willow sprigs between the flowers. The border is based upon a pattern weaving its way through *Daffodil*, a printed cotton designed by J H Dearle in 1891.

It is important to spend time at the beginning planning the pattern on the walls. The flowers are arranged in a grid pattern and, where possible, the flowers at the corners of a given square in the grid are all different. A blue sprig is stencilled in the middle of the square. Measure your walls and decide how far apart you'd like the flowers. Mark their positions, using a spirit level (carpenter's level) and plumb line to keep the flowers lined up. Before stencilling the

border, paint in a 2in- (5cm-) deep band (see page 23) around the top of the wall, ½in (1.2cm) from the ceiling, and along the skirting (baseboard) using the blue paint thinned with emulsion (latex) glaze. If desired, you can simply stencil a blue edge to this and omit the blue and pink edging and flowers.

To stencil next to the ceiling, or just beneath a windowsill, you will probably need to fold the top edge of the stencil. This will allow you to get right up to the edge, and will also protect the adjacent surface from paint. To get into difficult corners, either fold the stencil or cut a small stencil containing just a section of the border design, which will be easier to bend and move about.

When mixing the paints, vary the proportions to obtain lighter or darker shades. Add a little acrylic medium to the blue and the pinks to help the paint flow evenly and add translucency.

The step-by-step instructions given here are for stencilling the wall, but the technique for the flowers is the same when one of them is being stencilled onto a small object such as a lampshade.

MATERIALS
Acrylic medium
Emulsion (latex) glaze
Acrylic paints:
Pinks: cadmium red medium, white, raw umber, with extra white for the lighter pinks
Blue: cobalt blue, raw umber, white
Mauves: white, occasionally a little cobalt blue
Yellow: Naples yellow, white

1 *To stencil the border, position the pink border stencil so that the inner edges of the rectangles are along the edges of the painted band. If necessary, fold the top edge of the stencil. Apply pink through all windows.* **INSET:** *Replace with the other border stencil, positioning it so that the ties between the rectangles exactly cover the pink rectangles. Apply blue through all windows.*

2 For the mauve/yellow pansy, apply blue for the leaves and mauve for the outer portions of the petals, using a deeper mauve around the edges. Apply yellow to the centre so the colours just merge.

3 With the flower stencil still in position, hold one or two of the three cut-out centre pieces in place and apply a deep mauve over the yellow. Use the remaining centre piece(s) in the same way to complete the "stamens".

4 Use the cut-out pieces from the leaves to apply deeper blue centres to the leaves. Stencil the other flowers in the same way. Paint each carnation in light pink after removing the stencil.

OPPOSITE
Although this design is laid out on a grid pattern, it can be adapted to suit any space, from a large wall to a sloping ceiling.

RIGHT
For a lampshade or other small item such as a wastebasket, paint a narrow blue band around the top and bottom edges, then stencil on one or two flowers. To make it easier, tape the stencil securely in position on the curved surface, and wedge the lampshade firmly in place with cushions.

Enlarge all the templates for this project to 250 per cent (see pages 18–19).

Two interlocking stencils are used for the border, and one stencil for the blue sprig. There is a stencil for each of the four flowers. Both sides of the flower and sprig stencils are used. The cut-out centres of the pansy, aster and daisy flowers are used separately to stencil the centres of these flowers, as are the cut-out centres of the leaves of the aster and the base of the carnation flower.

Pink border piece

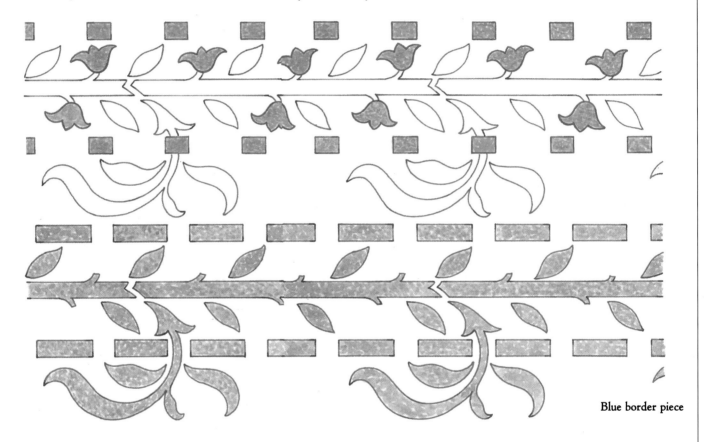

Blue border piece

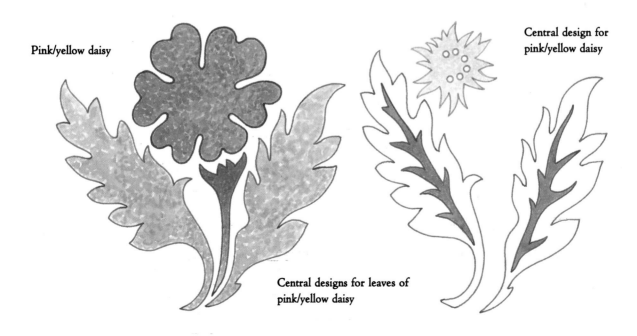

Pink/yellow daisy

Central design for pink/yellow daisy

Central designs for leaves of pink/yellow daisy

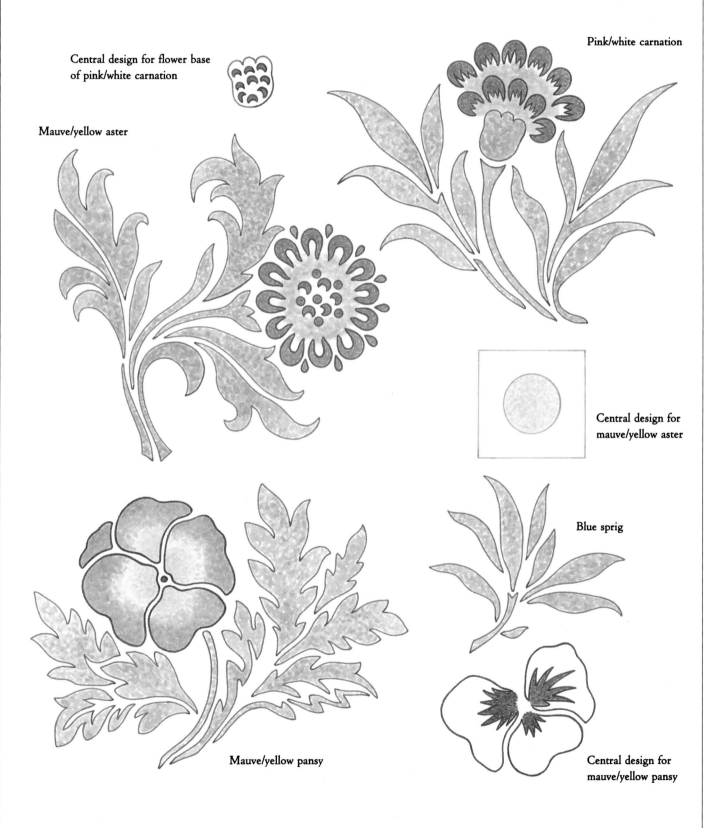

Central design for flower base
of pink/white carnation

Pink/white carnation

Mauve/yellow aster

Central design for
mauve/yellow aster

Blue sprig

Mauve/yellow pansy

Central design for
mauve/yellow pansy

Acanthus Mat & Cabinet

With their warm colours and flowing design, this floorcloth and matching cabinet will brighten up any bathroom – or kitchen, bedroom or hall. Inspired by a Voysey carpet, it is based on swirling acanthus leaves interspersed with forget-me-nots.

ABOVE AND OPPOSITE
The floorcloth and cabinet are linked in pattern and colour. Motifs from the floorcloth are used on the cabinet, but the colours are reversed. Most of the leaves on the floorcloth are the rusty-red of the cabinet itself rather than the brownish-yellow of the leaves.

This design comes from a carpet by C F A Voysey. Known for his light, elegant designs, Voysey had an enormous influence on the Arts and Crafts movement and also on Art Nouveau. An architect as well as a designer, he designed every detail of his houses, including carpets, wallpapers, fabrics and furniture. His designs generally incorporated stylized flowers, trees, animals or hearts.

The floorcloth shown here is 44 x 69in (112 x 175cm). Before stencilling it, you'll need to iron the canvas and paint it with two coats of white primer, leaving it to dry between coats. Tint the primer with ochre and raw umber acrylic paints to make it honey-coloured, and apply this roughly and thinly as a third coat.

When it is completely dry, turn under 1¼in (3cm) to the wrong side on all four raw edges of the canvas. Trim off a triangle at each corner within the turning to make the

corner flat. Glue the turnings in place with latex adhesive, using scissors handles to press them flat. When the glue is dry, the floorcloth is ready to be stencilled.

The cabinet was this rusty-red shade when purchased, but you could stain or paint a plain one, or alter the stencil colours to suit your cabinet. The step-by-step instructions given here are for the floorcloth; for advice on stencilling the cabinet, see the caption on page 101.

MATERIALS
White canvas
White water-based primer
Latex adhesive
Flat acrylic varnish
Acrylic paints:
For tinting topcoat: ochre, raw umber
For tinting varnish: raw umber
Red: cadmium red, red oxide, unbleached titanium
Yellow: Naples yellow, olive green, ochre
Royal blue: cerulean blue, unbleached titanium
Sky blue: cobalt blue, unbleached titanium
Orange: orange
Brown: raw umber

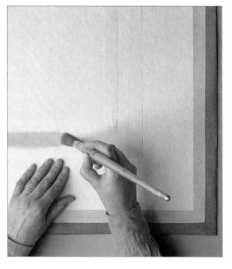

1 *Paint the canvas and make up the floorcloth. Lightly draw pencil lines ¾, 1½, 6¼, 7 and 7½in (2, 4, 16, 18 and 19cm) from the edges all around for the borders. Using masking tape, paint one red and two yellow ¾in- (2cm-) wide bands as shown.*

2 *Use the line stencil to add a royal blue border inside the inner yellow border. Soften the ends by fading the colour away just short of the end and then, before the paint has dried, repositioning the stencil so the ends just overlap.*

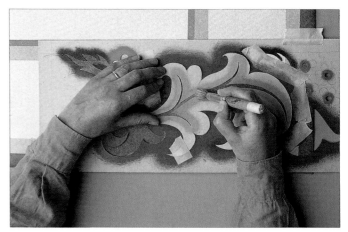

3 *Place the border stencil at the bottom right corner; the tips of the leaves will overlap both yellow bands. Mask out the unused part of the stencil at the corner, and any flowers that are very close. Stencil the two large leaves in red, then add brown shading around the edges to prevent the design from looking too flat.*

4 *Stencil the small leaf that is to the left of the flowers in brown. With the stencil still in place, lay the cut-out leaf centre on top of the stencil, positioning it exactly over the large leaf from which it was cut, and tape the stencil in place. Stencil the veins on the large leaf in yellow.*

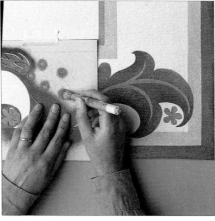

5 *Remove the cut-out centre and the masking from the flowers. Now mask the areas close to the flowers. Use the two blues to stencil the cornflowers, making some one colour and others a mixture.*

6 *Remove the remaining masking tape and move the stencil to the left so that the holes for the flower centres are positioned exactly over the flowers. Stencil the flower centres in orange.*

7 *Continue around the border. So that the motifs will be symmetrical, fill in corners with extra flowers and the corner motif if necessary. Now mask out the position of the leaves-and-flowers stencil in the centre.*

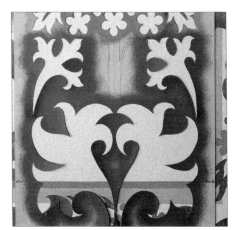

8 *Stencil the lower leaves in red, the flowers in sky blue and royal blue, and the upper leaves in yellow. Shade the lower edges of the red leaves and also the yellow leaves with brown.*

9 *Remove this stencil and replace it with the central stems-and-flower-centres stencil, in the same position. Stencil the flower centres in orange, the stems of the flowers in brown and the leaf veins in yellow.*

10 *Stencil the remainder of the centre portion of the floorcloth. You can, if you prefer, do this before step 9 so that you do not have to keep changing stencils. Apply three coats of flat acrylic varnish.*

ABOVE

The acanthus leaf predominates in this design. Widely used since early times, it was a favourite motif of William Morris and the Arts and Crafts designers. The feeling of movement is emphasized by the tips of the leaves overlapping the yellow borders.

LEFT

Before stencilling the cabinet, remove the knobs and rub it down a little with fine sandpaper. Hand-paint a thin blue line around the edge. Now stencil repeat images from the one stencil, flipping it over to use the reverse side on alternate boards, and stencilling the leaves and flower centres in yellow, and the flower petals in blue. Use the lower-edge motif to fill in yellow leaves along the bottom.

Enlarge all the templates for this project to 200 per cent (see pages 18–19).

The floorcloth border is stencilled using one stencil and a corner leaf stencil (plus the cut-out leaf centres for the leaf veins), with a line stencil for the blue inner border. The centre of the floorcloth is stencilled using two interlocking stencils – one for the leaves and flowers and one for the stems and flower centres. The cabinet is stencilled using both sides of another stencil plus a tiny motif along the lower edge.

Leaves and flowers for floorcloth central design

Stems and flower centres for floorcloth central design

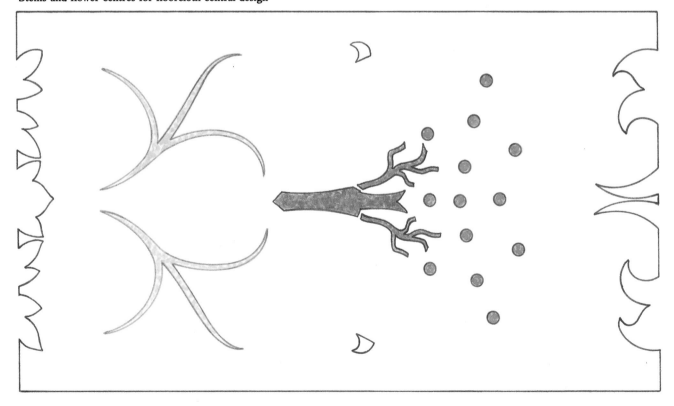

Leaves and
flowers for
floorcloth
border

Inner line for floorcloth border

Corner leaf design for
floorcloth border

Central design for
leaves of floorcloth
border

Main motif for cabinet

Motif for cabinet
lower edge

Camellia Bath Panelling

Simple bath panelling is here transformed by stencilling. Inspired by a painted sideboard by Philip Webb, each panel of the design consists of a pot of camellias and leaves, and the panels are surrounded by stylized foliage and individual flowers.

ABOVE AND RIGHT
Delicate shading and jewel-like colours characterize this lively stencilling. Although the shading is very subtle and can actually be omitted, it adds depth and interest to the work and makes it look much more elegant.

Rich shades of red, blue and turquoise are set against a suitably aquatic sea green in this design. It is based on a sideboard decorated with gilt leather panels and painted and ebonized wood, itself possibly inspired by Chinese lacquerwork. Designed in 1862 by Philip Webb, the sideboard was one of Morris's firm's best-selling designs.

The stencils used here are designed for panels measuring 18¾ x 11in (48 x 27.5cm) and 4in (10cm) apart. On the end of this bath, the panel is 25in (63.5cm) wide, so extra leaves were stencilled at the sides. The stencils could be enlarged or reduced, but it might be easier to start with plain, flat panelling and add mouldings.

Small portions of the flower-strip can be used individually as wall decoration.

A little acrylic medium may be added to the paints if desired, to help the paint flow easily.

MATERIALS

Emulsion (latex) paint in two shades of blue-green
Acrylic medium (optional)
Flat polyurethane varnish
Acrylic paints:
Dark red: prism violet, red oxide, Naples yellow
Blue: ultramarine, white, a little raw sienna, a little raw umber
Turquoise: viridian, cerulean blue

1 *Paint the panelling, using the lighter blue-green emulsion (latex) on the inner panels and the darker blue-green on the rest. Allow to dry. Place the main stencil in one of the inner panels, folding the edges so it fits exactly. Tape it in place. Use the dark red to lightly stencil the pot, making the colour stronger around the edge.*

2 *Place the cut-out piece back inside the pot and secure it in position with masking tape. Mask off any vulnerable windows if you wish, then stencil with the blue paint over the dark red to create the patterning on the flowerpot, applying the paint a little more heavily at the edges than at the centre.*

3 *Stencil in the leaves and stems in turquoise. To obtain a softly shaded effect, use slightly darker turquoise on some leaves than on others, and also use the darker shade on the edges of some leaves. You do not have to do this in a consistent manner – even random shading will add texture and interest.*

4 *Stencil the flower petals in blue, leaving the centres of the three middle flowers free of paint so that the blue-green background colour shows through. The flowers along the top edge are stencilled completely in blue. Use a little blue to shade the curved handle on the flowerpot and also the base of the pot.*

Flower strip

5 Add subtle shading to the flowers by stippling them lightly with dark red over the blue, being very careful to apply only a small amount of paint on the tips of the petals. A delicate touch is essential with this type of effect. (For a simpler stencil, this shading of the flowers can be omitted.)

6 Holding one of the cut-out flower centres in place with your fingertips, stencil the yellow centre on the flower through the cut-out circle. Repeat for the other two main flowers. Remove the whole stencil. Stencil the remaining panels in the same way, but don't worry if they do not match exactly.

7 Use the flower-strip stencil next, to stencil the flowers alongside the panels. Once again, you will need to fold the edges so that the stencil fits exactly into the space between the panels, and the edges of the moulding are protected from paint. Stencil the flowers alternately in turquoise and dark red.

8 Finally, use the leafy-strip stencil to add the leafy design above and below each of the panels. Stencil the leaves in turquoise, again using both lighter and darker turquoise for shading (see step 3). Stencil the three dots in dark red. When all the paint is completely dry, apply two coats of flat polyurethane varnish.

Leafy strip

*Enlarge all the templates for this project to
167 per cent (see pages 18–19).*

Panel design

*One stencil is used for the panels.
The cut-out centres for the pot and flowers
are also used; after the centres are cut from the
flowers, a small circle should be cut
out of the centre of each. There is a stencil
for the vertical area between panels, and
another for the space above and below the
panels. The templates should be joined
at the dotted lines.*

Central design for flowerpot

OUTDOORS

Stencilling doesn't have to be restricted to the inside of your home. The outside of the house and the garden offer excellent opportunities too. Bold, simple designs such as the stylized oak leaf on the planter (page 123) are well suited to the larger scale of nature. Stencilled only in terracotta shades, the planter will form an excellent background for flowers or plants. The wooden bench (page 112), on the other hand, has an intricate and flowing design typical of Arts and Crafts designs. Stencilled in two strong colours, it would be ideal for brightening up a shady corner or patio. Both projects use oil-based paint and yacht varnish to provide maximum weather resistance. For items that will sit on a porch or be kept in a shed when not in use, such as the director's chair (page 120) or the trug (page 117), this obviously is not a factor. Other items you could stencil for the garden include a window box, shutters, deck chair, slatted wooden chair, parasol, painted brick wall, or even the door of a shed.

Rabbit & Porcupine Bench

Arts and Crafts flora and fauna grace this colourful garden bench. The rabbit design on the back is derived from William Morris's Brother Rabbit *fabric, while the porcupines running along the seat edge are from a cabinet by William Burges.*

ABOVE AND RIGHT
Rabbits crouch among the leaves while porcupines march in an orderly procession in this whimsical design. Although the rabbit and porcupine motifs are derived from different sources, their style is very similar and they work well together.

William Morris's *Brother Rabbit* fabric, upon which this stencil design is based, was Morris's tribute to the Uncle Remus stories about Brer Rabbit. First published in the United States in 1879, these stories were an instant success and were particularly enjoyed by the Morris family.

The *Brother Rabbit* fabric was first hand-blocked in 1882. It was initially printed in indigo, and later in a deep, soft red – which are the two colours used in this stencil.

The rabbit which recurs in the design (and which looks nothing like Brer Rabbit) is actually by Philip Webb, who drew the animals in many of Morris's designs. A leading architect and designer who was closely associated with Morris's company for most of his life, Webb had a particular talent for drawing animals. He explained, "To draw animals you must sympathize with them; you must know what it feels like to be an animal."

Like Philip Webb, William Burges, who designed the cabinet from which the porcupine in this design is taken, was an architect and designer. The leading exponent of the Gothic Revival style of architecture and furniture, Burges designed colourful, richly decorated painted furniture that was heavily influenced by medieval designs. He was extremely knowledgeable about the Middle Ages and drew upon medieval sources for the porcupine. The cabinet is a good example of the delight in colour and fantasy that is apparent in his exquisitely painted furniture. It is now in the William Morris Room at the Victoria and Albert Museum in London.

This stencil is ideal for a long shape like a garden bench, but the rabbit could also be used singly on a cushion or a little table. A line of porcupines could run along a skirting (baseboard) or the motif could be used individually on a notebook or trinket box.

You may need to reduce or enlarge the rabbit stencils slightly to fit your bench. Similarly, you may wish to space the porcupine motifs further apart.

When mixing the paint, add a little acrylic medium to the blue, and an even smaller amount to the red, to make it a pliable consistency.

MATERIALS

Oil-based undercoat or exterior paint in yellow
Acrylic medium
Yacht varnish
Oil-based signwriter's (Japan) paints:
Blue: ultramarine, Prussian blue, Payne's grey, white
Red: crimson, red oxide, ultramarine, white

1 *Paint the bench with two coats of undercoat. Measure the back, and mark in pencil where each repeat will be positioned. Tape the rabbit stencil in place at one end. Because the pattern is intricate, you may wish also to use spray adhesive on the back of the stencil – in which case use it only in a well-ventilated area.*

2 The cut-out pieces of the rabbit from the stencil are used as a mask to prevent blue paint from being smudged onto the rabbit. Position the mask over one rabbit and tape it in place or hold it with your free hand as you stencil. Stencil the leaves in blue, softening the paint (p 23, step 1) before you get to the edges.

3 Remove the rabbit mask but not the stencil. When the blue is dry, use a different brush to stencil the edges of the leaves red. Now use the blue brush to brush over where the red and blue meet so that the edges blend together. (There is no need to take up any more paint, as there will be enough residual paint on the brush.)

4 *With the stencilling brush that you used for the red paint, stencil both rabbits in red. Hold the stencil down with your fingers if you are not using spray adhesive, and take care to get the paint right into the narrowest parts of the stencil. You might find that you need to add a drop more of the acrylic medium.*

5 *Use the cut-out portion of the rabbit's head, with the eye shape cut out from it, to stencil a blue eye on each rabbit. You can use the same brush for this as for the blue leaves. The blue is stencilled on top of the red, though you may need to apply two coats of paint in order to make it show up enough.*

6 *Tape the porcupine stencil to the front edge of the seat. Stencil the porcupines in blue. Stencil only a little of the half-porcupine on the edge of the stencil, then use this as a placement guide when you reposition the stencil to continue along the edge of the seat. If desired, use the cut-out shape to add red eyes and ears.*

7 *Paint red stripes above and below the line of porcupines on the front of the seat. Here the stripes were painted freehand using the shape of the wood as a guide. If there are no suitable guide lines on your bench, you will need either to draw faint pencil lines with a ruler first or to use masking tape (p 23, steps 2 and 3).*

8 *Use the leaf stencil to stencil blue leaves on the seat. These are simplified versions of the leaves on the back of the bench and therefore do not have any red on the edges. They should look scattered, so position them randomly, at different angles, and sometimes with the stencil turned over.*

9 *Place the same stencil lengthwise on one armrest. Tape it in place and then stencil in blue, as for the seat. Turn it over to stencil the other armrest. Finally, apply two coats of yacht varnish to the entire bench. This very tough varnish doesn't chip and will protect your work from the weather.*

*Enlarge all the templates for this project
to 167 per cent (see pages 18–19).*

Rabbit motif

*For this design there is a rabbit
stencil and a rabbit's head cut-out.
A porcupine stencil is used along
the front of the seat, with the
cut-out used for eyes and ears if
desired, and a leaf stencil
on the seat and arms.*

Porcupine motif

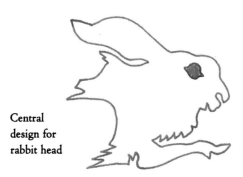

Central
design for
rabbit head

Central design for
porcupines

Leaf motif

Green Pastures Garden Trug

Taken from a carpet border by C F A Voysey, this bucolic design of a line of shepherds is highly appropriate for a rustic wooden garden basket. The design has been changed very little from Voysey's original carpet border.

ABOVE
Voysey's shepherds – complete with crooks, clay pipes, smocks, hats and boots – adapt well for use as a border stencil. The ties emphasize these details and add to the overall character of the motif, while the stencilled stripes serve to frame the shepherds.

The border that inspired this stencil design is from an Axminster carpet by C F A Voysey, one of the leading architects and designers of the late nineteenth and early twentieth centuries known for his light, elegant style. Voysey called his design *Green Pastures* and it is a good example of the humour and originality of his work. Woven in 1896, the carpet is thought to have been exhibited at that year's Arts and Crafts Exhibition.

Voysey's designs for carpets, textiles and wallpapers were dominated by repeat motifs and pastoral subjects like this. Though often deceptively simple and rustic, with a strong narrative quality rather like nursery images, they demonstrated a control over pattern and an economy of line that were very subtle. His light touch and freshness prompted the Art Nouveau artist Van de Velde to say of Voysey's early work, "It was as if Spring had come all of a sudden."

In this stencil design the line of shepherds encircling the trug is very similar to the line of shepherds ranged around the edge of Voysey's carpet. The stripes around the base and around the handle of the trug echo those on either side of the carpet border.

The border can be stencilled onto any trug with flat wooden sides. The pastoral theme also makes it suitable as a border on a tablecloth for the garden, a wooden window box, a canvas picnic rug, the edge of a flat window blind (shade) or a canvas tote bag.

MATERIALS
Emulsion (latex) paint in sky blue shade
Flat polyurethane varnish
Acrylic paints
Orange: orange, a very small amount of red oxide, white

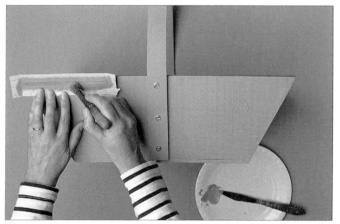

1 *Paint the whole trug with sky blue emulsion (latex), applying it straight onto the wood. When it is dry, hand-paint the upper edge orange. Now use the single-line stencil to apply an orange line around the sides near the top, aligning a pencil line on the stencil with the top edge to keep the orange line straight.*

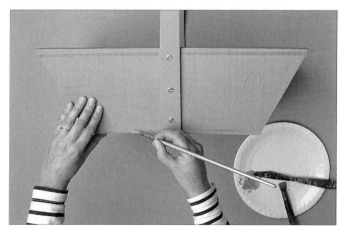

2 *Repeat the procedure along the lower edge, first painting the bottom edge orange by hand and then stencilling an orange line parallel to this. The distance between the two lines should be the same as that between the two lines along the top edge. This stencilled line will represent the ground.*

117

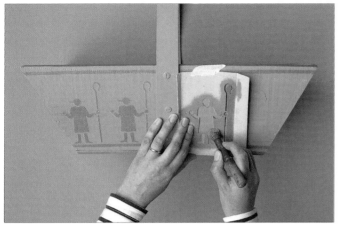

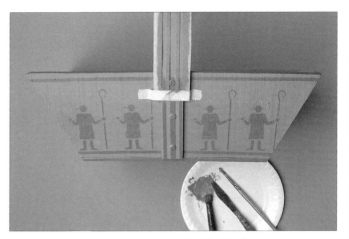

3 *Plan the placement of each repeat. Tape the stencil in the first position, avoiding having the shepherd's feet right on the line. Stencil in orange then reposition the stencil and repeat, folding the side edge of the stencil when working near the handle. Continue until all four sides are stencilled.*

4 *Finally, tape the three-line stencil to the handle, centring it between the edges. Stencil the three lines in orange, leaving the ends soft (p 23, step 1). While the paint is still wet, reposition the stencil so that the ends overlap, then continue stencilling the lines. Carry on in the same way around the handle. Varnish.*

Enlarge all the templates for this project to 167 per cent (see pages 18–19).

OPPOSITE

The trug can be painted in any combination of colours prior to stencilling, or it can be stained or left natural, depending upon how rustic an effect you would like. If you don't wish to use it in the garden, it would also look nice filled with pine cones or, appropriately, balls of knitting wool.

The main stencil consists of one shepherd, which is repeated around the trug. A single-line stencil is used for the inner line at top and bottom, but the outside lines are hand-painted. The handle is stencilled using a three-line stencil.

Three-line border

Shepherd motif

Single-line border

Tulip Border Director's Chair

Use a simple but striking design such as this stylized tulip border to liven up a canvas director's chair. It is taken from a tile border designed by William de Morgan, who was himself influenced by Islamic patterns.

ABOVE AND OPPOSITE
This stylized border of bands of tulips can be used as a conventional edging but it works particularly well repeated across a rectangular area. As well as being stencilled onto a canvas chair, it could be used on a tablecloth, on curtains, or as a border around a small room.

William de Morgan, who designed the tile border upon which this stencil is based, was a lifelong friend of William Morris, and a leading ceramicist and tile-maker to whom Morris's firm often sub-contracted work. Heavily influenced by Islamic pottery, de Morgan based this design on Turkish tulip tiles. His masterly use of stylized bird, animal and plant motifs and rich carefully integrated pattern had a major influence on the Arts and Crafts movement and also on Art Nouveau. He is said to have done for ceramics what Morris did for wallpapers.

Although de Morgan intended his design to be used for border tiles, it has a timeless quality that makes it seem just as appropriate today. It is particularly well suited to the simple lines and colourful canvas of a director's chair. One contrasting colour will look better than two or more – simplicity is the keynote here.

The seat and back are stencilled in the same way. The easiest method of marking out the positions of the stencils is to mark the centre of the seat or back and then cut out four strips of paper the size of the finished border pattern. Lay two of these where the outer stencilled bands will be (in other words, just inside the stitching on each side). Now space the other two equally between them, checking that they are the same distance either side of the centre mark on the canvas. Mark with tailor's chalk. If you are using acrylic paints, add a little fabric medium to make the paint a better consistency for stencilling on the canvas.

MATERIALS
Fabric medium (if using acrylics)
Tailor's chalk
Acrylic paints or fabric paints:
Dark purple: burnt umber, prism violet, Payne's grey

1 *Remove the chair seat and back from the frame. Using tailor's chalk and strips of paper the same size as the stencil, mark where each of the four bands will go. At the bottom of the band, mask off the lower parts of the leaves on the stencil if necessary to make it fit. (This will depend on the size of your chair.)*

2 *Place the stencil in the first position, and secure with tape. Protect your work surface, as you will be stencilling right up to the edge. Apply paint through all windows, leaving the ends of the stripes soft (p 23, step 1). Reposition the stencil and add two dots at the bottom using a small brush.*

Tulip border

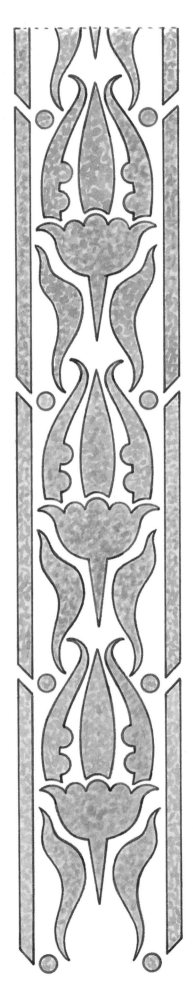

3 While the paint is still wet, use a small "line" stencil to fill in the ties in the stripes on both sides of the bands of tulips. Doing this before the paint has dried will help to prevent the stripes from looking uneven, since the areas of paint will blend into each other when wet, but not when dry.

Enlarge the template for this project to 167 per cent (see pages 18–19).

One stencil is used for the repeated bands of tulips on the seat and back of the chair. A small line stencil should be made from this stencil, to use for filling in the ties.

4 Position the stencil along the marked lines for the next band and stencil in the same way, taking care not to smudge the previous band. Once again, fill in the ties while the paint is still wet to maintain uniformity. You will see the design beginning to build up into an all-over pattern over the canvas.

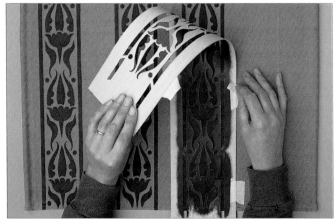

5 Repeat the procedure for the remaining two bands. Be sure always to peel the stencil away carefully to prevent smudging. Paint smudges cannot be repaired on fabric and would be very noticeable in such a dark colour. (If you do get a smudge, leave it to dry then try to scrape it away with a razor blade.)

Oak Leaf Wooden Planter

Based on a New York stained-glass window, this stylish wooden planter looks good stencilled in the colours of nature – grey-green and terracotta. For a rougher effect, rather like driftwood, you could stencil in soft white onto unpainted wood.

ABOVE
This simple oak leaf design is stencilled onto the grey-green painted wood background using a terracotta shade, with touches of a slightly deeper terracotta for textural interest. The circles within the design are echoed by a circle at each corner of the planter.

The design of this stencilled planter came from a stained glass window attributed to Charles Booth, in Calvary Church, New York. Booth, an English stained-glass artist, took the Aesthetic design principles of Christopher Dresser with him to America, where a new design movement was underway influenced by William Morris and all that was happening in the Arts and Crafts movement in England.

The oak leaf design is a good example of Booth's and Dresser's preference for strong geometrical forms. The simple bold outline and stylized plants adapt well to a stencil design and are ideally suited to a sturdy, square-sided planter like this – although the design would also make an excellent stencil for floorboards.

The paint should be of a fairly dry consistency. Oil-based signwriter's paints (Japan paints or bulletin colors) have

been used here; not only are they waterproof but they are also faster-drying than most other oil-based paints. You could use acrylics instead of oil-based paints if you varnish the planter afterwards (which will not only help to protect it but also enhance the colours).

Yacht varnish is the longest-lasting, but flat polyurethane would be suitable too. If you have used signwriter's paints and do not wish to varnish the planter, you could simply leave it to weather naturally.

MATERIALS
Exterior paint in dark grey-green shade
(flat finish if possible)
Yacht varnish or flat polyurethane varnish (optional)
Oil-based signwriter's (Japan) paints or acrylic paints:
Light terracotta: raw sienna, burnt sienna, Naples yellow
Dark terracotta: raw sienna, a little more burnt sienna,
Naples yellow

1 *Paint the planter all over with the exterior paint. Enlarge or reduce the design if necessary on a photocopier so it will fit your planter. Cut the stencil so there will be enough margin on each edge to fold up and protect the planter edge from smudges. Position it on the recessed panel, taping it in place if necessary.*

2 *Make sure that your brush and the paint are both quite dry. Using a circular action, apply the light terracotta shade through all the windows of the stencil. Apply the paint fairly thickly. You may need to apply a second coat to ensure adequate coverage over the dark grey-green background.*

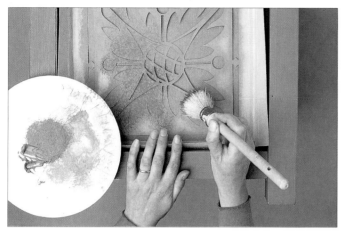

3 *When the paint is dry, carefully stipple on a little of the dark terracotta shade in places, holding the brush at right angles to the planter. Avoid using a circular action here – the aim is to just lightly touch the surface in places, creating an interesting, gently dappled or mottled effect.*

4 *To stencil each corner dot, position the circle stencil so that the dot is centred; mark the outer edges of the planter on the stencil. Apply the light terracotta and then add a touch of the dark terracotta. Repeat the procedure at the other corners, lining up the stencil lines with the edges of the planter.*

Enlarge both templates for this project to 167 per cent (see pages 18–19).

Main oak leaf design

OPPOSITE

The bold shape of the oak leaf design is strong enough for a chunky planter like this, while the paint colours allow it to blend with the grey-greens of foliage and the terracotta shades of brickwork and clay pots.

On each side of the planter, use the main stencil on the recessed panel, and the circle stencil at the four corners.

Corner circle

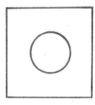

Index

Acknowledgements

Being involved in this book has been a rewarding experience – especially getting to know William Morris more fully. I have had a wonderful team to work with, and I would especially like to thank Alison Wormleighton, who has calmly guided me through this book and skilfully rewritten my scribbled notes; Lucinda Symons for her wonderful photography, and Mary Morrison for making the photo sessions good fun; Lucy Elworthy for the beautiful props and styling; Carol McCleeve for her inspired design; Steve Gott for his splendid sets; Sarah Hoggett for her encouragement and Philippa Lewis for her excellent picture research, as well as her suggestion that I should "do" this book, for which I am most grateful. Thanks also to Andy Vargo for his help, and Norwich Art School Library for the long loan of invaluable books.

In addition, I would like to thank Peter Heward of Classic Finishes, 150-162 King St, Norwich NR1 1QH, tel 01603-760374; Daler-Rowney Ltd, Bracknell Berks RG12 8ST, and Liquitex UK, Binney & Smith Europe, Ampthill Rd, Bedford MK42 9RS, for supplying paints used in the projects; and the following for the loan of props: David Mann & Roger Belston, Stiffkey Lamp Shop, Stiffkey, Wells-next-the-Sea, Norfolk NR23 1AJ, tel 01328-830460; Richard Scott Antiques, 30 High St, Holt, Norfolk; and Geeta Maude Roxby.

The publishers would like to thank the following, who kindly lent props featured in the photographs: pp 28-9, 39 (upholstered armchair, kilim): George Smith, 587-589 Kings Road, London SW6 2EH, tel 0171-384 1004; p 31 (coatstand, table, mirror, chair, wall lamp, vase): Zeitgeist, Kensington Church St, London W8; p 51 (iron curtain pole): The Bradley Collection, The Granary, Flowton Brook, Flowton, Suffolk, tel 01473-652651; p 51 (Sussex chair): New Century, tel 0171-937 2410; p 51 (Arts and Crafts lamp): The Stiffkey Lamp Workshop, as above; p 55 (white metal planter, terracotta pot): The Chelsea Gardener, tel 0171-352 5656; pp 80-1, 83 (side tables): Mary Maynard Antiques, tel 0171-731 3533; p 94 (bedspread and cushion): Chelsea Textiles, tel 0171-584 1165; p 99 (basin, taps, towel rack, planter): The Water Monopoly, 16/18 Lonsdale Road, London NW6 6RD, tel 0171-624 2636; pp 104-5 (bath, taps, candle sconces, mirror, bath rack): The Water Monopoly, as above.

All the photographs in this book were specially taken by Lucinda Symons for Collins & Brown Limited with the exception of the following: pp 6 and 12 (top): author's collection; p 8 (right): private collection; p 10 (right): National Trust Picture Library; p 11 (top): Victoria & Albert Museum, London; p 13 (bottom): Christie's Images.